A present from Opa and
Oma for your christening
at 30-11-2008

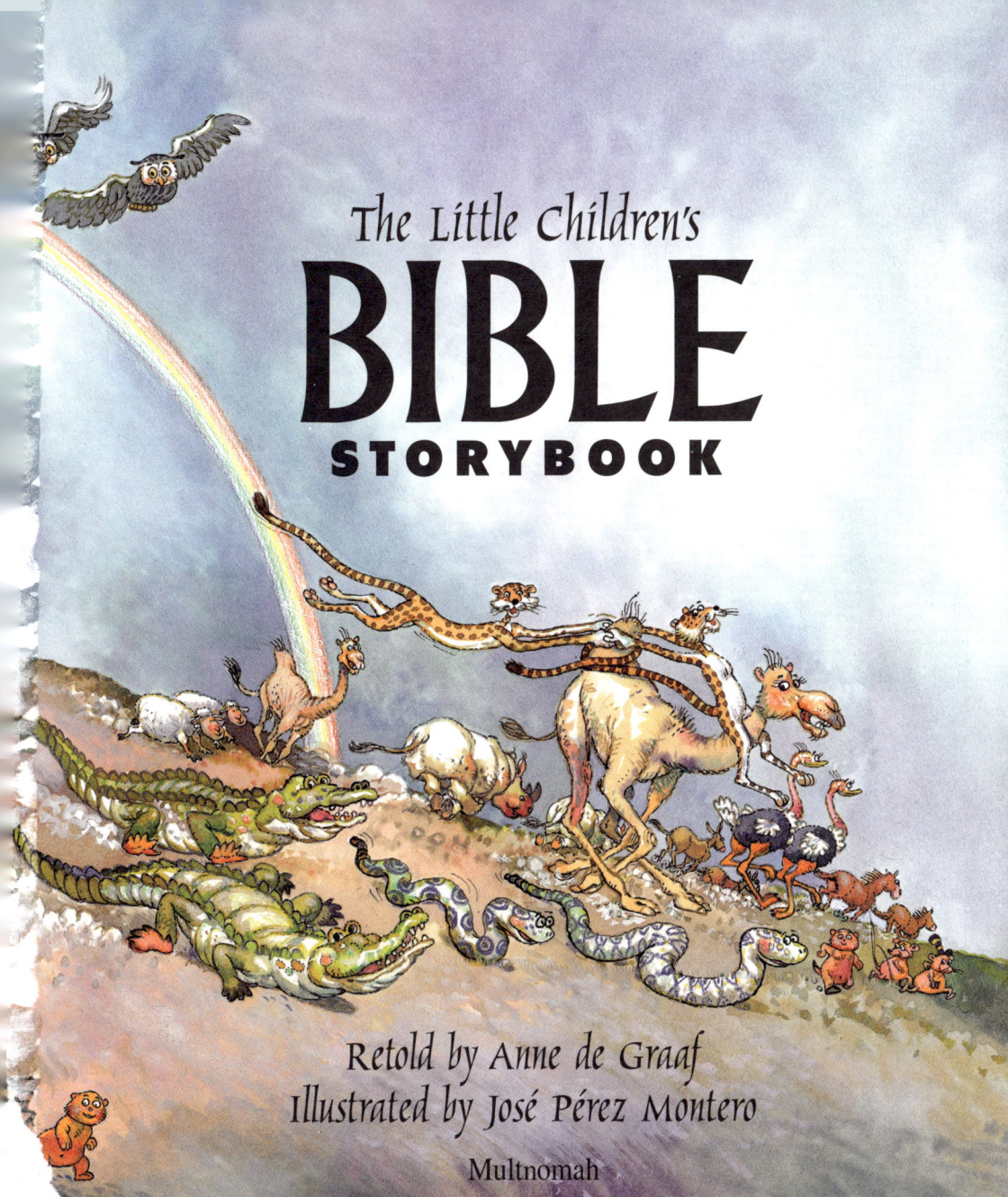

The Little Children's Bible Storybook

Copyright © 2002 Scandinavia Publishing House, Drejervej 11-21,
DK 2400 Copenhagen NV, Denmark. Tel.: (45) 35310330   Fax: (45) 35310334
E-Mail: jvo@scanpublishing.dk

Text copyright © 2002 Anne de Graaf
Illustration copyright © 2002 José Pérez Montero
Design by Ben Alex

Printed in China
ISBN 15 9052 606 6

All rights reserved. No part of this book may be reproduced or utilized in any form or by any means, electronic or mechanical, including photocopying, recording, or by any information storage and retrieval system, without permission in writing from the publisher.

A Note to the Big People

The Little Children's Bible Storybook may be your child's first introduction to the Bible, God's Word. This is a **DO** book. Point things out and ask your child to find, seek, say, and discover.

Before you read these stories, pray that your child's little heart would be touched by the love of God. These stories are about planting seeds, having vision, learning right from wrong, and choosing to believe.

In this **DO** book, wave, wink, hop, crawl, or do any of the other things the stories suggest so this can become a fun time of growing closer. Pray together after you read this. There's no better way for big people to learn from little people.

A little something fun in italics is said by each narrating animal to make that particular story come alive.

A Note to the Little People

Someone very special gave you this book. It is a special book, and it was given to someone even more special . . . and that's you.

This may be your first Bible. The Bible brings you closer to God. Even closer. Why even closer? Because Jesus said the angels of the little ones (that's you) are the closest to God.

There are lots of fun things to do when you hear these stories. Listen closely. Your job is to make sure the someone special who reads to you does these fun things with you. After that, you can both close your eyes and thank Jesus for being together. There's no better way for little people to learn from big people.

Table of Contents

The Old Testament

God Makes the World	pages 9–19
The First People	pages 20–29
Noah and the Ark	pages 30–41
Noah and God's Promise	pages 42–49
Noah and God's Gift	pages 50–61
The Beginning of the Tower of Babel	pages 62–75
The End of the Tower of Babel	pages 76–89
Abraham Follows God	pages 90–97
Abraham's Great Big Family	pages 98–107
Joseph and the Colorful Coat	pages 108–115
Joseph Forgives His Brothers	pages 116–127
Moses Hears the Call of God	pages 128–139
Moses Leads God's People	pages 140–147
General Joshua and the Promised Land	pages 148–159
Gideon and the Fleece	pages 160–173
Samson the Super Strong	pages 174–187

Ruth Must Find a New Home	pages 188–197
God Rewards Ruth's Loyalty	pages 198–211
God Chooses David	pages 212–223
David Fights Goliath	pages 224–235
Solomon Saves a Baby	pages 236–245
The Wisdom of King Solomon	pages 246–255
Elijah the Prophet	pages 256–269
Jonah Tries to Run from God	pages 270–283
Jonah and the Big Fish	pages 284–297
Daniel the Prisoner	pages 298–309
Daniel and the Lions	pages 310–319
Esther the Beautiful	pages 320–327
Queen Esther Saves Her People	pages 328–335

The New Testament

Mary and Joseph	pages 337–347
The First Christmas	pages 348–361
The Miracles of Jesus	pages 362–369
Simon Peter the Rock	pages 370–383
The Stories of Jesus	pages 384–395
Children and Jesus	pages 396–403
Jesus in Jerusalem	pages 404–415
The First Easter	pages 416–427
Paul's Change of Heart	pages 428–435
God Promises a New World	pages 436–447

THE OLD TESTAMENT

God Makes the World

Genesis 1

*Close your eyes.
Hold your breath. Shhhh.*

There was nothing in the beginning. . . except for God.

God, who is the Source of light, took the darkness and changed it so that suddenly . . .there was light.

The light came from the sun. God made the earth and moon, all the planets and the stars.

God made the oceans and the seas. He made fish, and more and more and more fish.

God made the land. He made animals, and more and more and more animals.

The First People

Genesis 1–3

God made the world. Then He made the first man and called him Adam. God made a helper and friend for Adam and named her Eve.

Just like He made you, your fingers, your toes, your smile, too.

Adam and Eve lived in a special garden called Eden. God had one rule: not to eat the fruit from one tree. God said, "No." The serpent told Eve, "Yes."

Eve chose to break the rule and so did Adam. This was wrong.

What rules do you know?

When Adam and Eve did not listen, they had to leave Eden. They never, ever felt as close to God again.

God went on loving Adam and Eve, though. No matter what, He always loves. God gave two sons to Adam and Eve.
Every child is a
gift from God.

A long, long, long, long time ago, no one said *Thank You!* to God anymore.

Everyone chose to be bad and this made God very sad. One man was different. His name was Noah.
Noah loved God and listened to Him.

Name all the things and people you can say Thank You! *to God for.*

God told Noah, "There will be a huge flood. Build a boat. Build a BIG boat. Build a VERY BIG boat!" Noah's boat was called an ark. Noah's neighbors laughed at Noah. "We live in the desert! Where's your water?"

Whom did Noah listen to? Whom do you hear now?

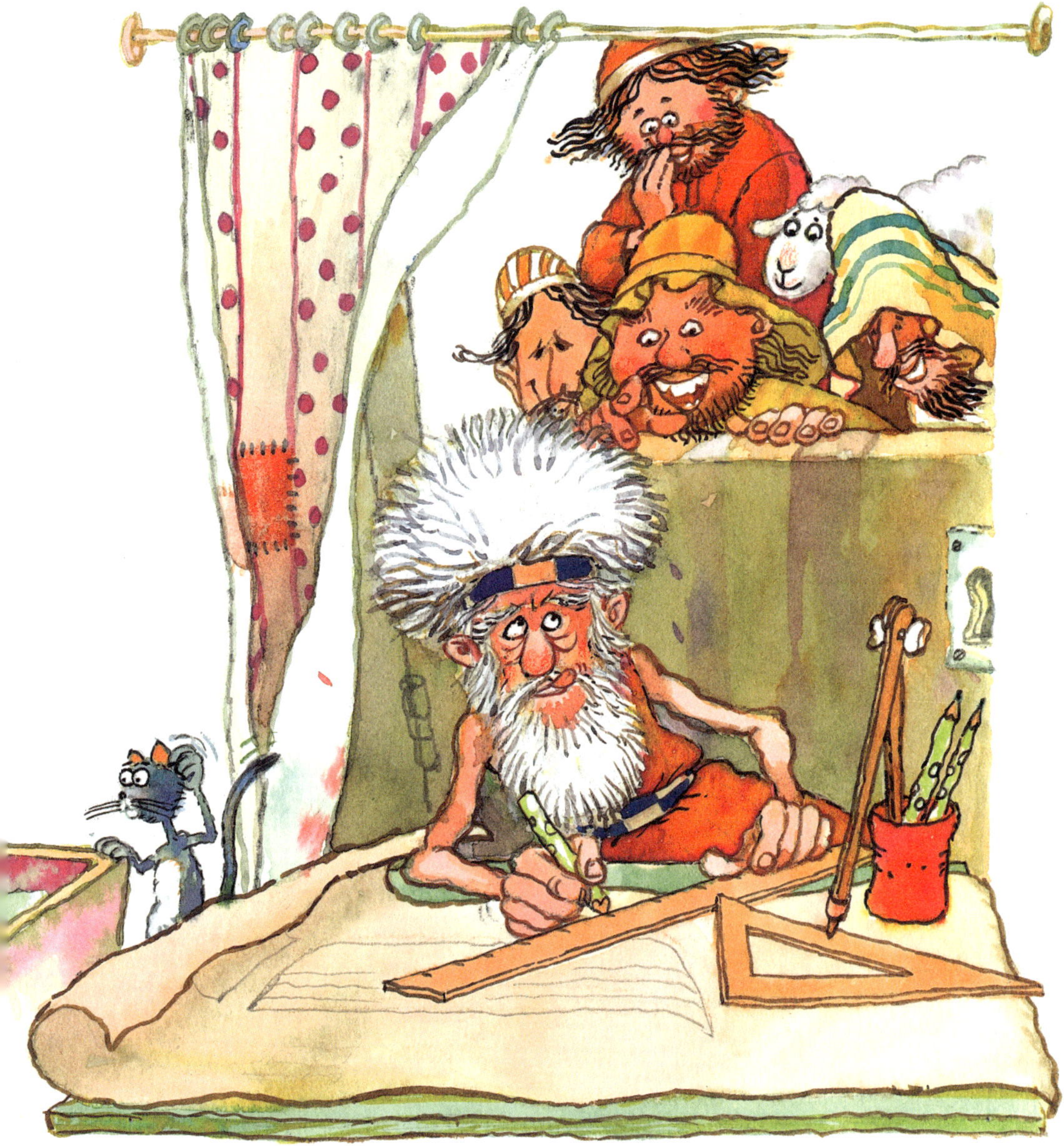

God said to fill the boat, the BIG boat, the VERY BIG boat with two of every animal. God promised to keep Noah and his family and the animals safe inside the ark.

How many different animal noises can you make?

Then it started to rain and rain.
It rained for forty days and forty
nights. All those animals! All
those days and nights! All
that rain!

Count your fingers. Count your toes. Do it all again. That's how many days it rained and rained and rained.

Noah's ark floated higher and higher, higher even than the mountaintops. As water covered the earth, all the living things of the earth drowned.

Finally the rain stopped.
Then God sent a wind.

*Make a sound like the rain.
Now make a sound like the wind.*

Noah and God's Promise

Genesis 8

Water was everywhere! Noah sent a raven to look for dry land.

Noah and the animals in the ark waited and waited for the water to go down. After the raven, Noah sent out a dove. TWICE!

Can you make flapping sounds like a bird? TWICE!

The second time, the dove returned with an olive branch in its beak. This meant that somewhere there were places dry enough for trees and plants to grow.

God said to Noah, "You, your family, and all the animals may leave the boat. Go onto the land and build homes."

47

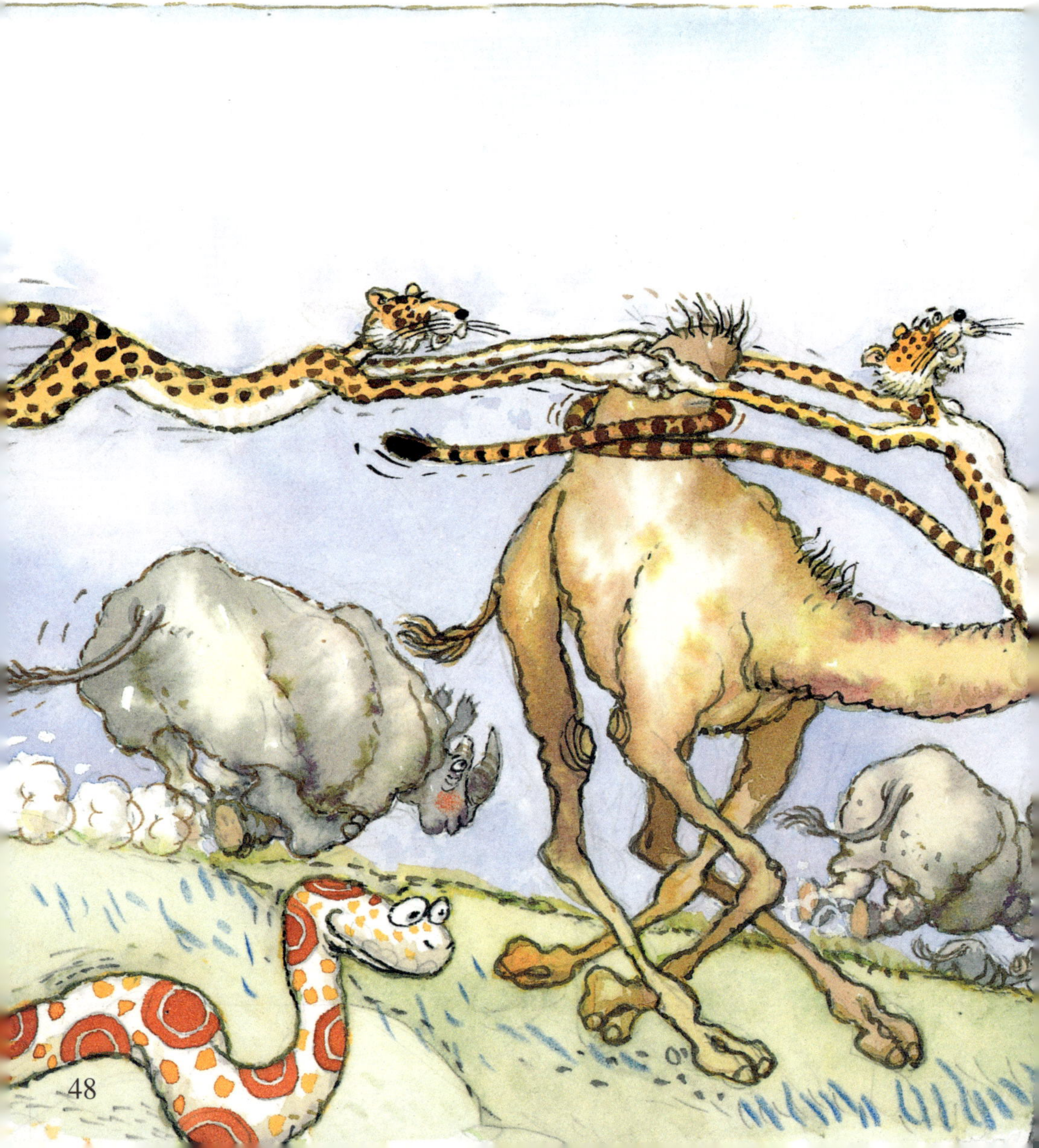

God kept his promise. He kept Noah and his family and all the animals safe and sound.

> *Show how the kangaroos got off the ark. And the snakes? Do you think there's more to this story?*

Noah and God's Gift

Genesis 8–9

Noah thanked God for keeping them safe. Then God gave Noah a gift.

Turn the page and see the present...

God gave Noah the present of another promise. God was so happy that Noah said *Thank You!* He promised three things.

First, never to flood the earth again.
Second, that there would always be
seasons of the year.

After autumn would come winter and after winter would come spring...

... and what comes after spring?

The third part of God's promise was that day would follow night.

. . .would follow day would follow night would follow day would follow night. . .

Then God made something very special. Using every color, He made the first rainbow. "As a sign of My promise, I have set My rainbow in the clouds."

How many colors are in the rainbow? Light blue, light-light blue...

God's gift to Noah, and to us, is the rainbow. This is God's sign that He always keeps His promises.

Just as the colors are endless, so the rainbow is endless. And just like the rainbow, God's love goes on and on and on...

The Beginning of the Tower of Babel

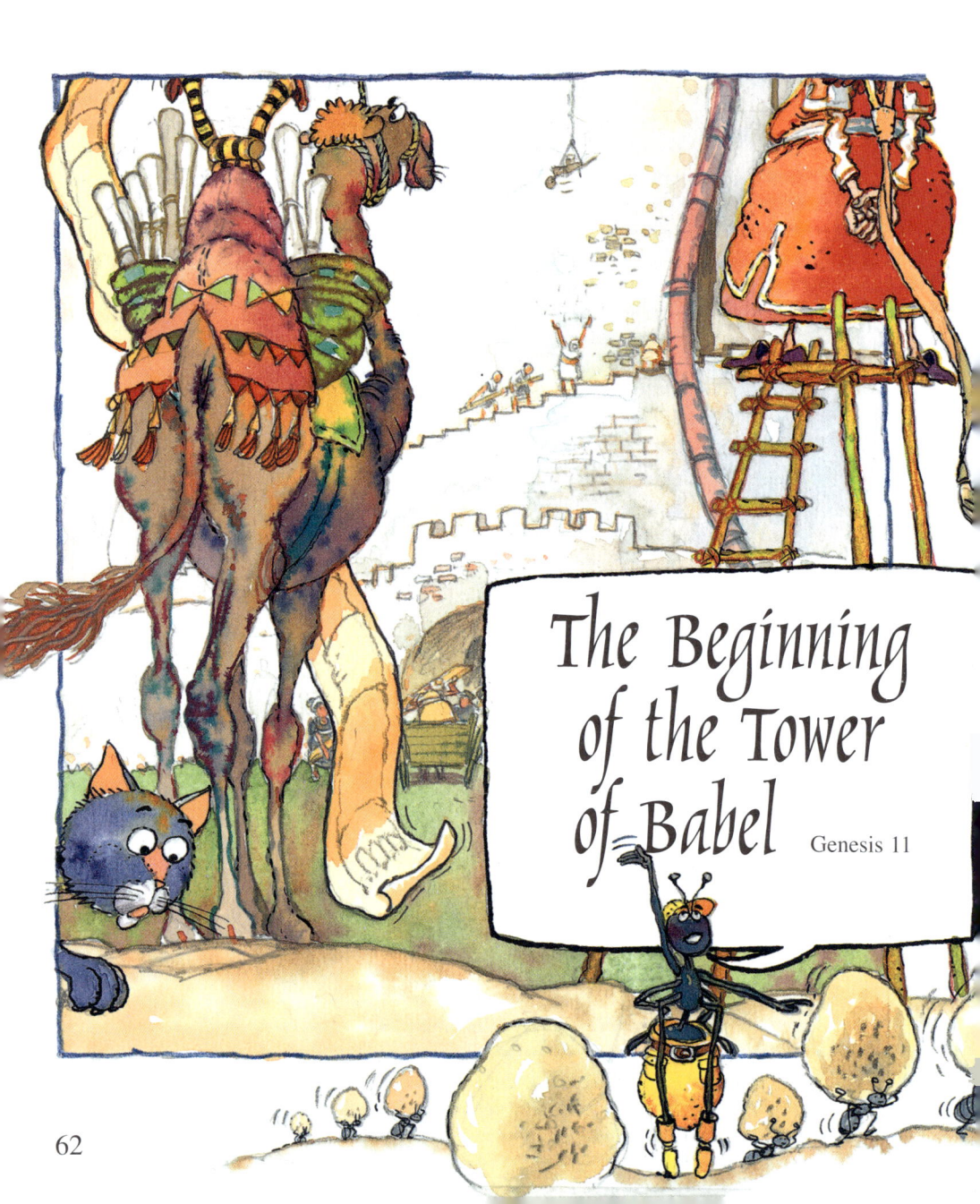

Genesis 11

63

What country do you live in? What language do you speak? "Mhoro!" is how you say hi in Shona, a language of Zimbabwe.

*If you're from Poland, you say,
"Czesc!"
And in Mexico, "Hóla!"*

A long, long, long time ago, everyone spoke only one language.

We speak the same language. Say "hi!" Say it louder! I hear you and say "hi!" back.

67

A long, long, long time ago, as people spread out to live, they still understood each other.

Hey you! Pick up that grain of sand! No, not that one, THAT one! He knows what I mean.

69

Then some people found a flat place and decided to make it their home.

I like flat places. They are easy to build on. The next time you play in the sand, clear a flat place before you build your tower.

The people said, "Let's make bricks and bake them until they're very hard."

What happens when you kick a tower made of sand? Whooosh! What happens when you kick one made of bricks? Ouch!!!!

The people were clever. Instead of using stones they made these bricks, and stuck the bricks together with tar, instead of mortar.

Build a tower with your fists, one on top of the other, on top of the other, on top of the other... Where will it stop?

The End of the Tower of Babel

Genesis 11

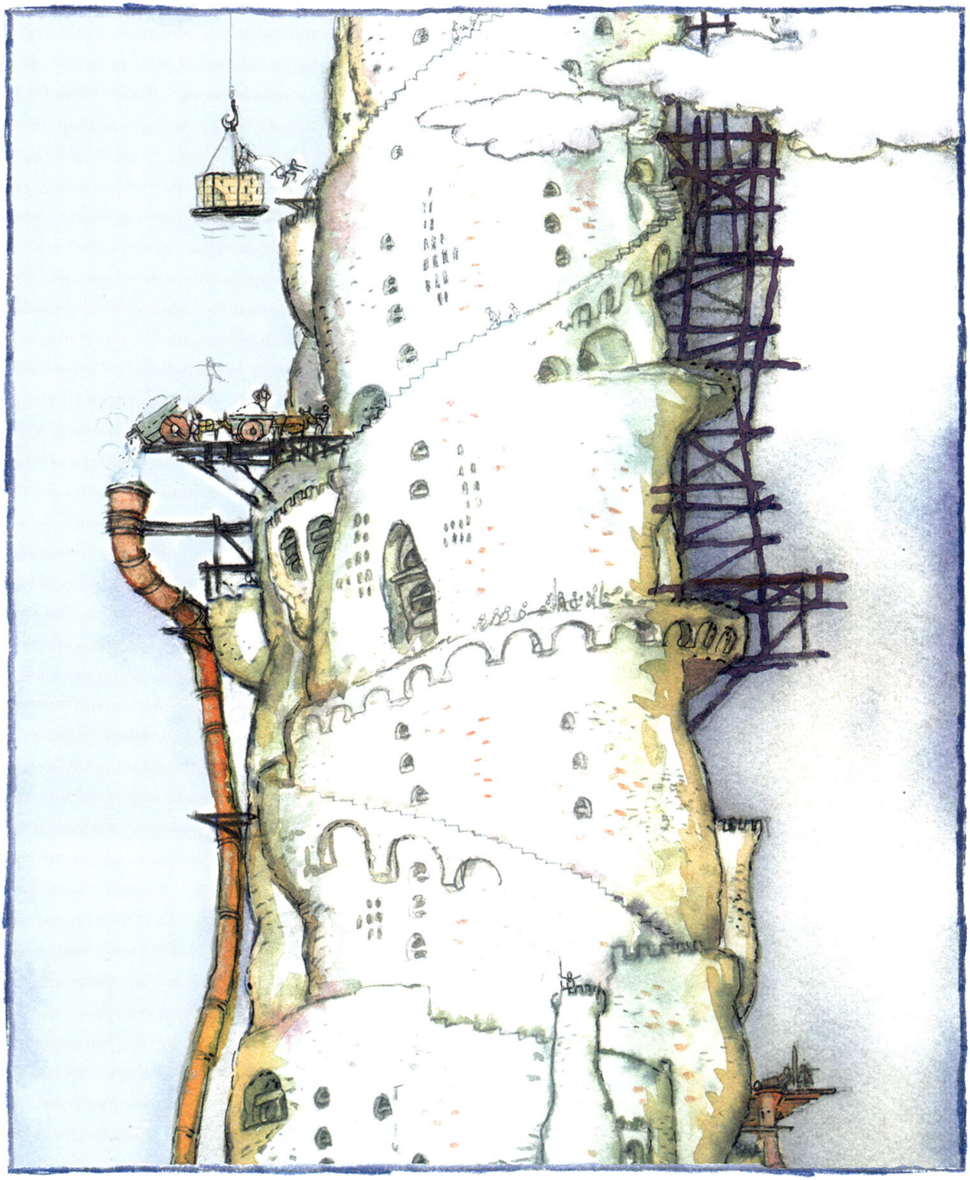

Oh, yes! The Tower of Babel was looking up!

These people said, "We can be famous and not have to wander anymore."

Then the people said, "Come, let's build ourselves a city! We will finally have a home."

Now a tower wasn't good enough. They had great plans!

When God saw what the people were trying to do, He knew He must stop them, or they would think they were gods.

They grew way too proud of themselves and their plans for a great tower and great city.

So God mixed up their words and made different languages. The people no longer spoke one language, but many.

Heavens! If workers don't understand each other, I could say, "Get that grain of sand!" and he might think I meant, "Hand me the hammer!" That's no way to build something.

85

The city they never finished building was called Babel, which means *Mixed Up and Confused*, because there the Lord mixed up the language of the whole world.

No matter how high you reach, or how big you dream, thank and praise God for helping you. Always include God in your plans.

Then the Lord sent all the people wandering, spreading them out all over the earth.

Adiós!
Czesc!
Chisarai zvakanaka!

Abraham Follows God

Genesis 12–13, 17

Abraham and Sarah loved God very much. Abraham means Father of Many. Sarah means Princess.
Baa! Do you know what your name means?

Abraham had many sheep, cattle, and camels. He and Sarah lived in the desert and slept in tents.

Don't forget the goats! How many goats with beards can you count?

94

One night, God told Abraham He would make Abraham's family into a great nation.

Abraham believed God and trusted Him. What nation are you a part of?

God also promised Abraham and Sarah a new homeland. So they packed their tents onto camels and traveled until God told them when and where to stop.

Pack your bags! Who's the leader here?

97

Abraham's Great Big Family

Genesis 13, 15, 17–18, 21

*Many years went by and Abraham and Sarah STILL didn't have a child. They asked God why.
How many stars are there?
A billion? This is how great and big a family God promised Abraham and Sarah.*

One day, three strangers visited Abraham and Sarah, who served them their best food. One of the visitors said Sarah would soon have a son.

More than anything else, Abraham and Sarah wanted a baby, a child just like you.

Sarah was listening from inside the tent. She laughed because she was now very old, too old to have a baby.

The visitor said, "Why did Sarah laugh? Nothing is too hard for the Lord to do."

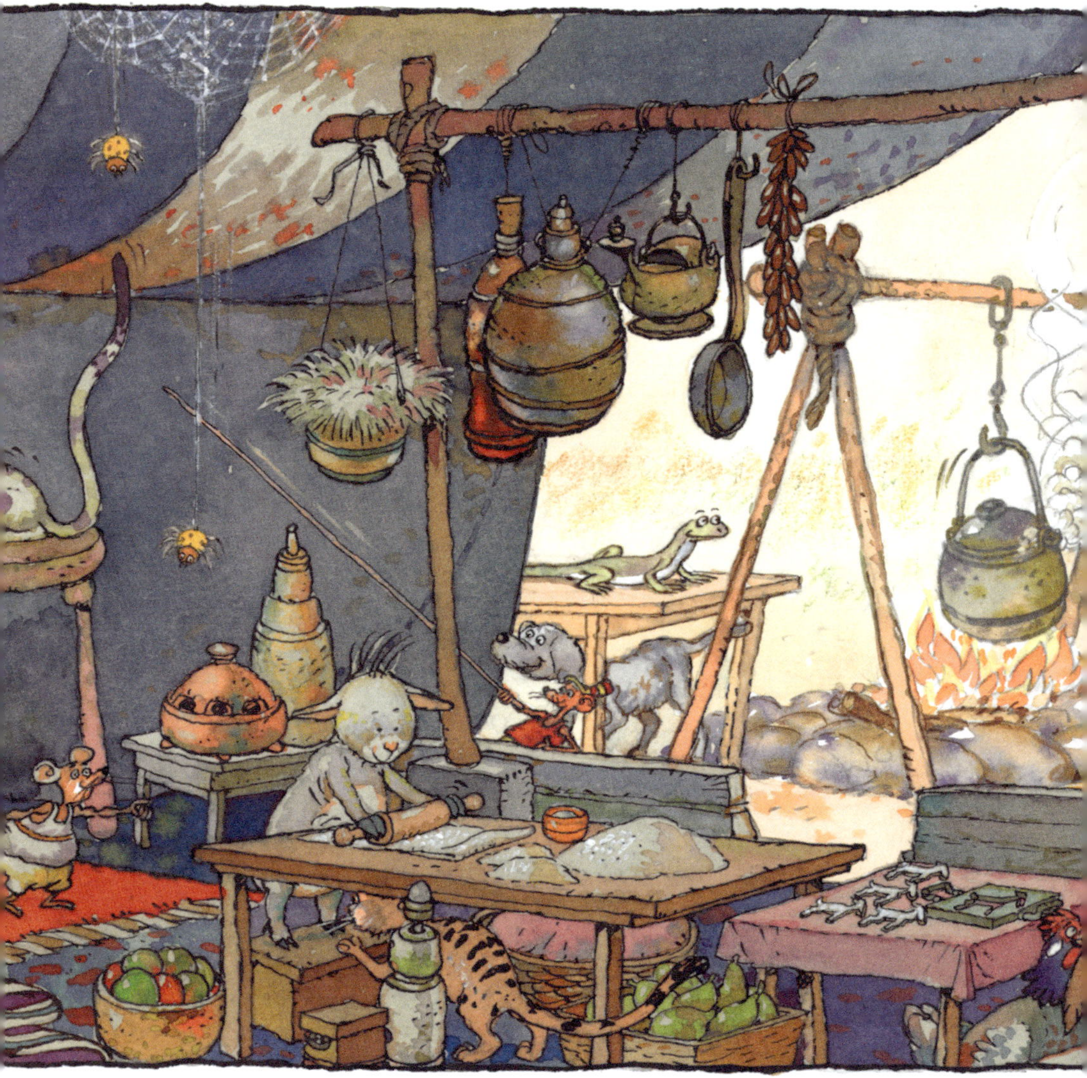

Sarah doubted what she heard. But Abraham knew the message was from the Lord.

A year later, Abraham and Sarah finally had their little boy, Isaac, God's own gift. Isaac was the beginning of the great big family God promised Abraham.
Isaac means *Laughter*.

Whom did Isaac make happy when he was born? Whom did you make happy when you were born?

107

Joseph and the Colorful Coat

Genesis 37

Isaac had a son named Jacob. And then Jacob had twelve sons. Joseph was his favorite. One day Jacob gave him a colorful coat. This made the other brothers jealous.

Have you ever had a dream? What did you dream about?

One night, Joseph dreamed the sun and moon and eleven stars bowed down to him, as if he were a king. His older brothers did not like this. "We'll never bow down to YOU!"

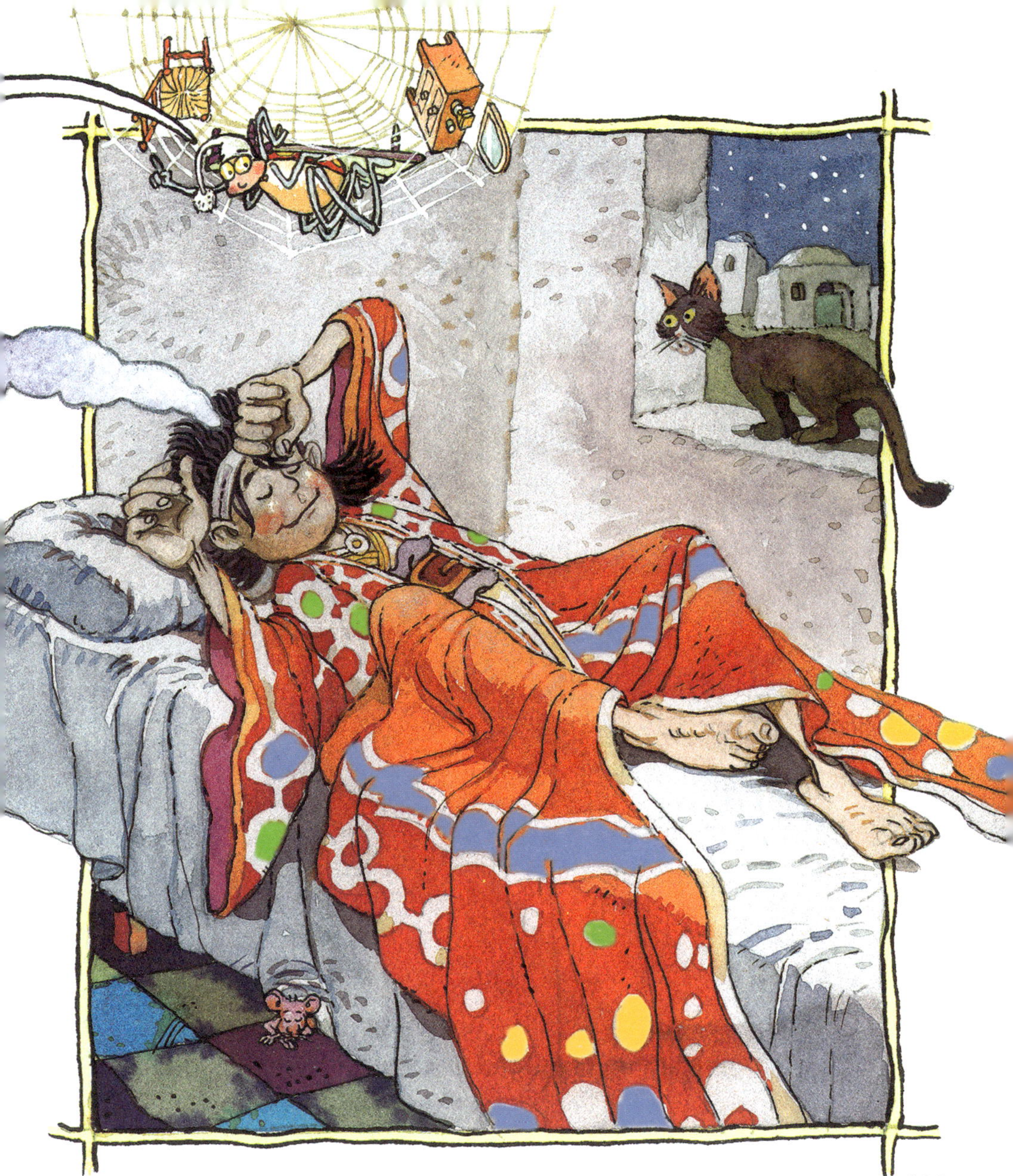

Joseph went to check on his brothers who were watching over the sheep. His brothers took his special coat and threw him in a well.

*Why would the brothers do this?
Should Joseph ever forgive them?*

Joseph's brothers sold him as a slave to Egypt, far, far away. But God was with Joseph.

Slaves are not free as a kite, like you and me. Where is Joseph's coat of many colors now?

Joseph Forgives His Brothers

Genesis 39–46

Joseph worked very hard as a slave in Egypt. The man who owned Joseph put him in charge of his home and farm. Joseph worked for God and thought of him as his REAL Master. What did you work hard at today?

In Egypt, God helped Joseph see what dreams meant. Pharaoh, the king of Egypt, told Joseph about a dream where seven fat cows crossed the river.

Then seven skinny cows crossed and ate the fat cows, but they still stayed skinny!

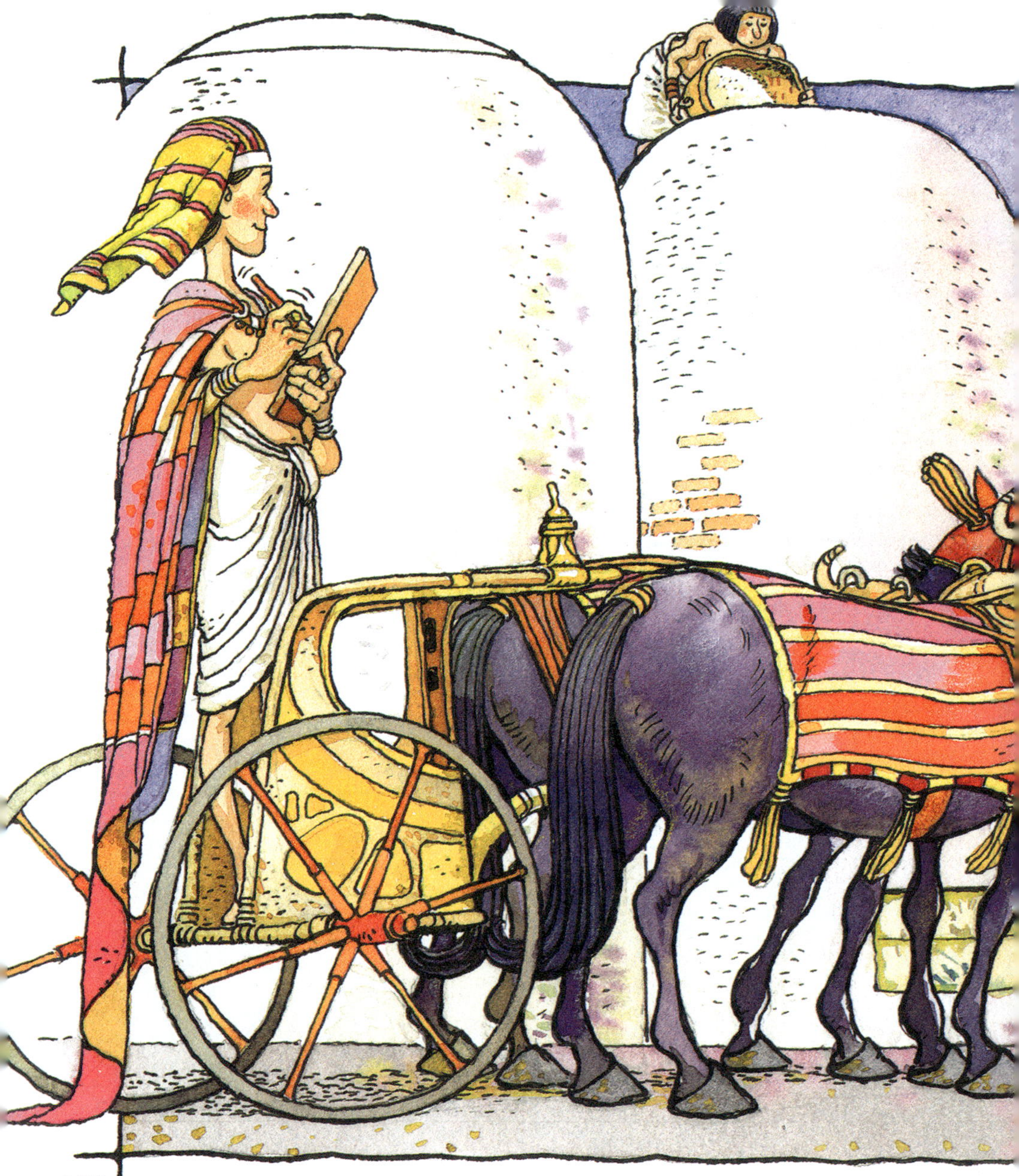

God showed Joseph that the fat cows meant seven good years. So Pharaoh freed Joseph and put him in charge of storing food.

After the seven good years came seven bad years. That's what the skinny cows stood for! Because it was so hard to find food then, Joseph's brothers came to Egypt. They did not recognize Joseph, but Joseph recognized them.

When Joseph looked into their eyes, he could not be mad at his brothers. What color are the eyes of the person reading you this story?

Joseph forgave his brothers for the mean trick they had played on him so long ago. God had taken care of Joseph. That was all that mattered. The brothers jumped for joy at finding each other again!

Have you ever been
mad at someone?
Did you forgive them?

Jacob and his sons moved to Egypt to be near Joseph. Now their family was together again!

Does your family have some favorite colors?

Moses Hears the Call of God

Exodus 1–4

A long time ago, when Moses was a little baby, much smaller than you, his mother saved his life.

The king of Egypt, or Pharaoh, wanted to hurt Hebrew babies like Moses. So his mother put him in a basket and sent him floating down a river.

God kept Moses safe. Pharaoh's daughter heard Moses crying. She saved him and made Moses her own son.

Moses grew up in the palace. The Egyptians hated Hebrews, who were God's people. One day, Moses saw an Egyptian hitting a Hebrew man. Moses killed the Egyptian and ran away.

Moses hid in the desert for many years in a place called Midian.

Moses married a woman from Midian. One day when he was tending his father-in-law's sheep, Moses saw a bush on fire, but the fire was not really burning the bush! How could that be?

It was God, trying to get Moses to listen!

135

What was God calling Moses to do? To go back to Egypt and help save God's people from the Egyptians. But Moses was afraid and said, "Not me, God."

Was Moses afraid?

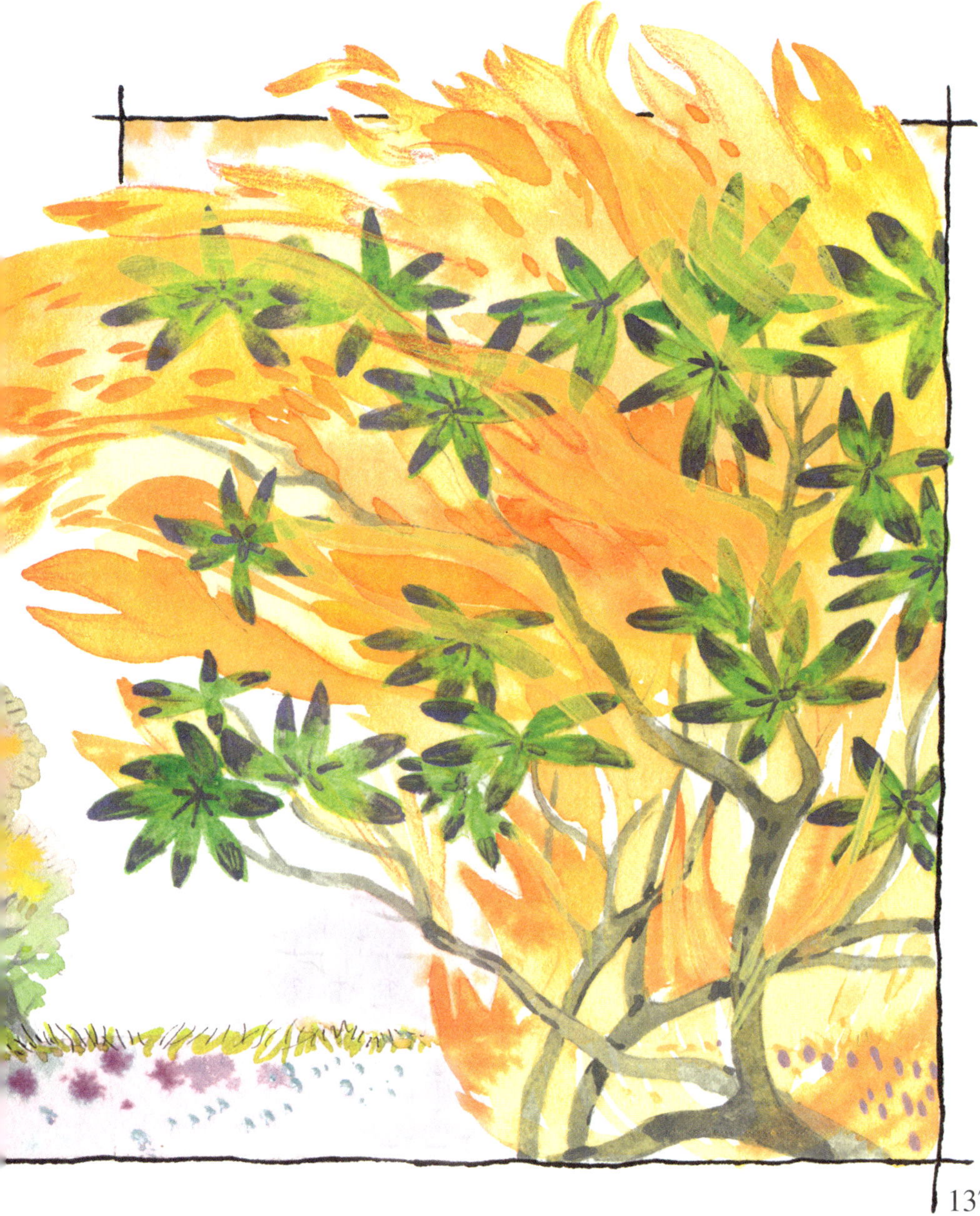

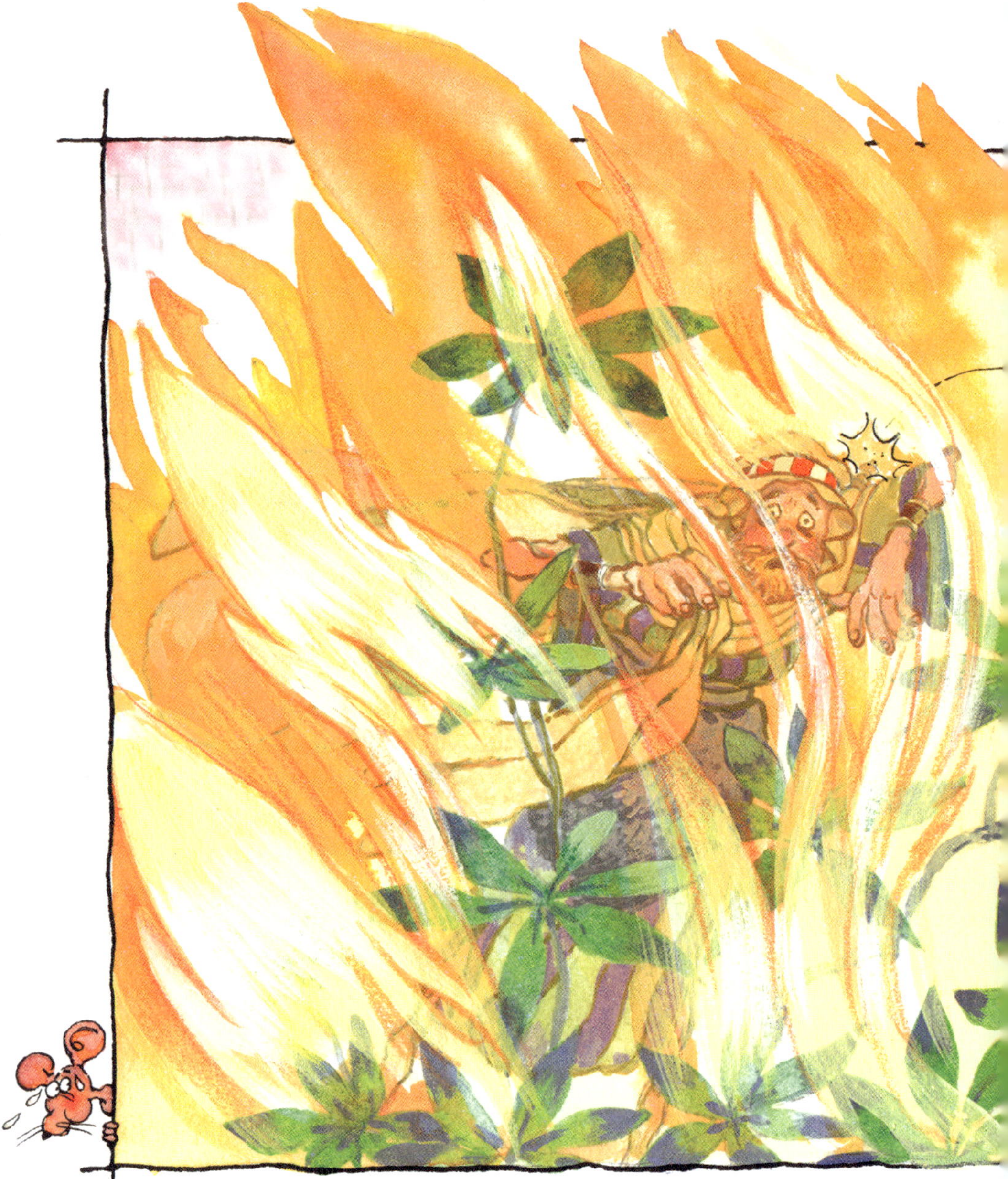

God knew Moses could not talk well, but God said He would fix that. All Moses had to do was listen to God's call and just say, "Yes."

How easy is it to just say "yes"? Do you ever find it hard to obey?

Moses Leads God's People

Exodus 5–16, 19–20, 33–34;
Numbers 13–14;
Deuteronomy 1

Moses led the people out of Egypt. Then God split the Red Sea right in half!

Moses obeyed God and returned to Egypt. He asked Pharaoh to release God's people. But Pharaoh's heart was hardened, and he said, "No!" God showed His power in many ways until finally Pharaoh gave in. Later, Pharaoh changed his mind. He cried out to his soldiers, "Go after them and bring them back!"

But God was watching over His people. Just as Moses' group reached the Red Sea, God made the waters split open! They all reached the other side safely before God closed the waters again.

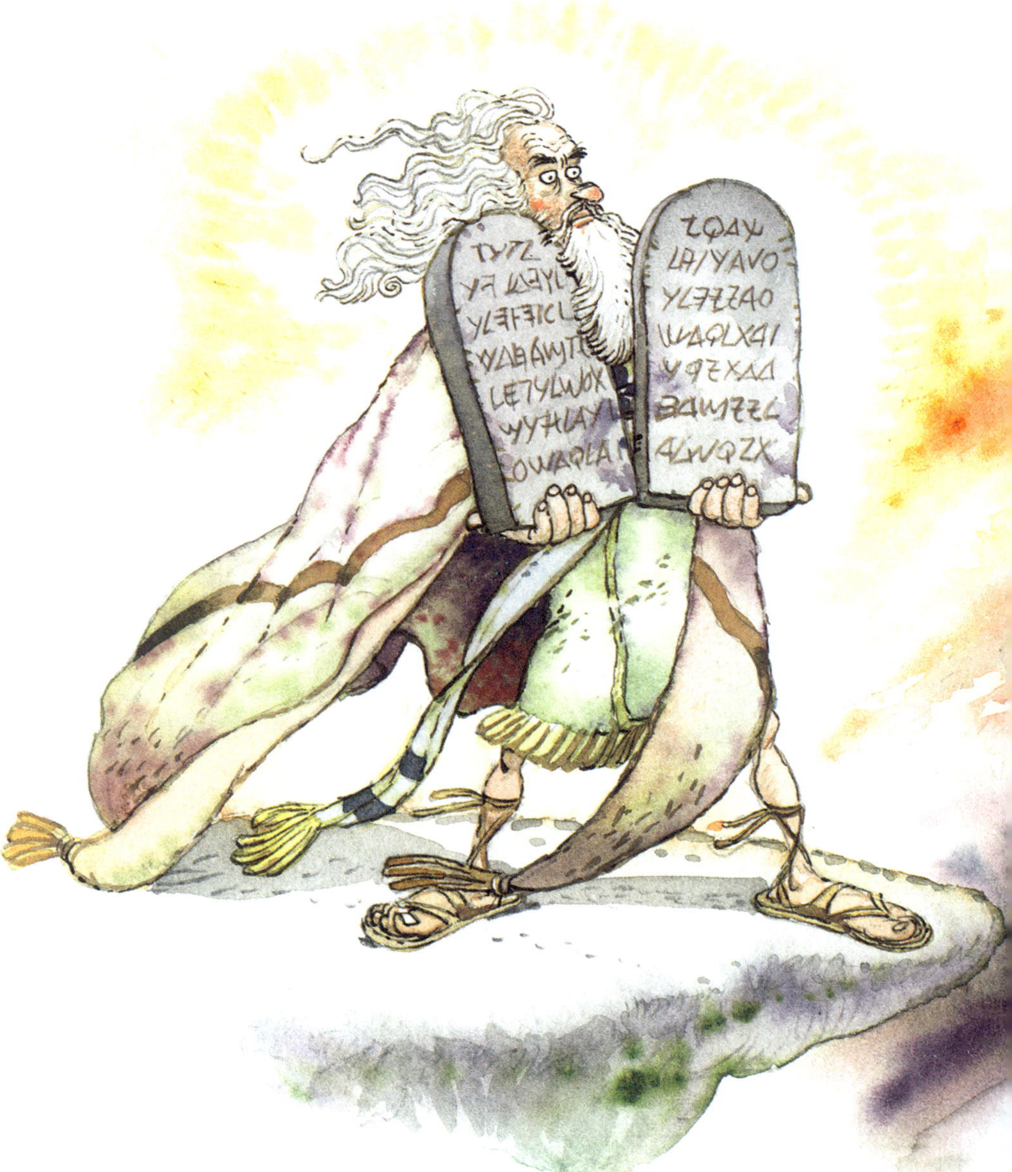

During the long journey to the Promised Land, God's people started to forget to praise and worship God. So God wrote in stone ten rules for Moses and his people to follow.

God gave these rules to keep His children safe, healthy, and happy.

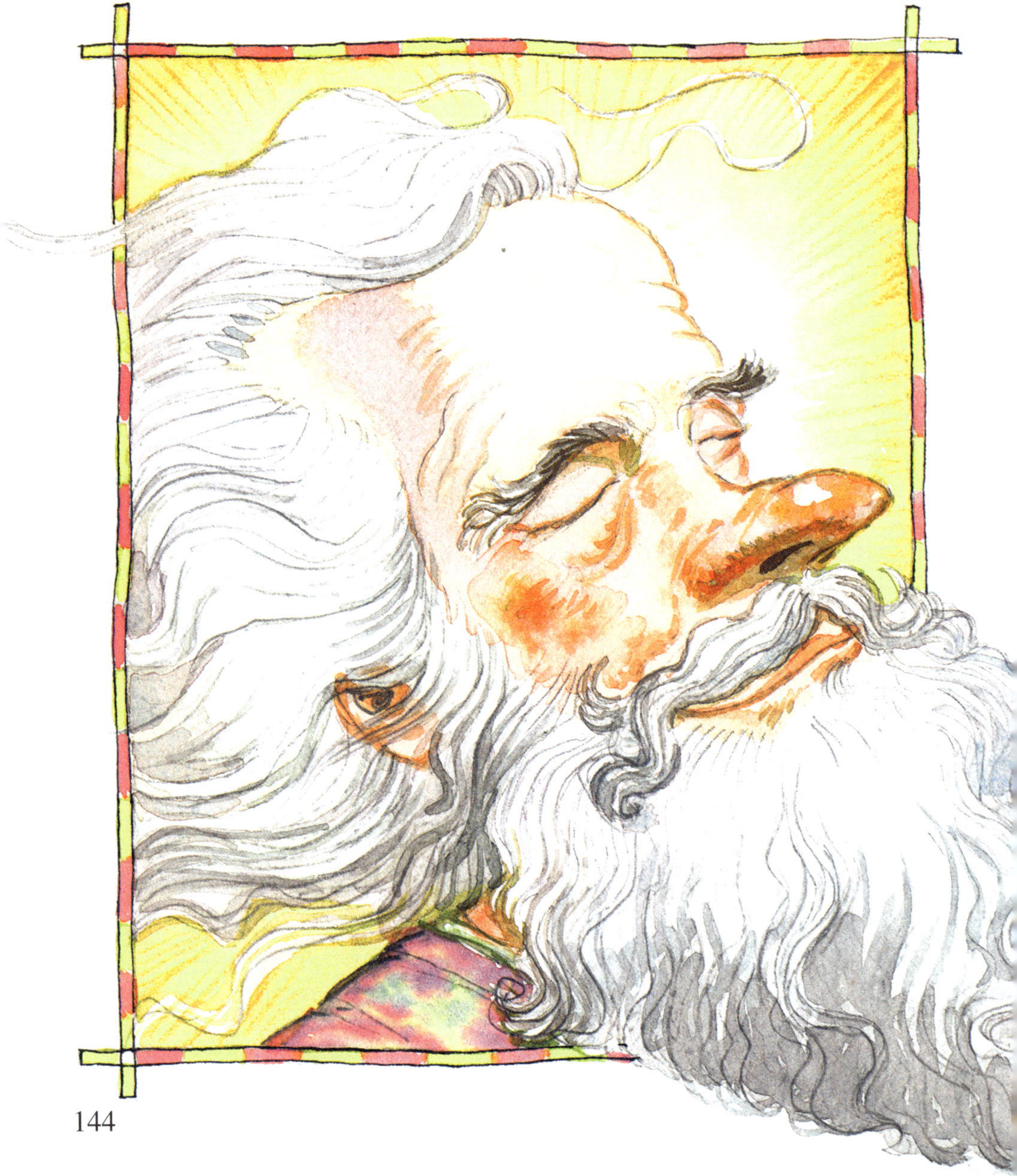

God gave these ten rules, or Ten Commandments, to Moses on a mountain. God spoke to Moses out of a thick cloud. His glory was so great that Moses shut his eyes tight.

Close your eyes and shine a light on your face. What does it feel like?

Have you ever heard your stomach grumbling? That's what God's people did in the desert— they grumbled!

It took God's people forty years to reach God's promised land, called Canaan. Despite their grumbling, God gave His people food and water every day.

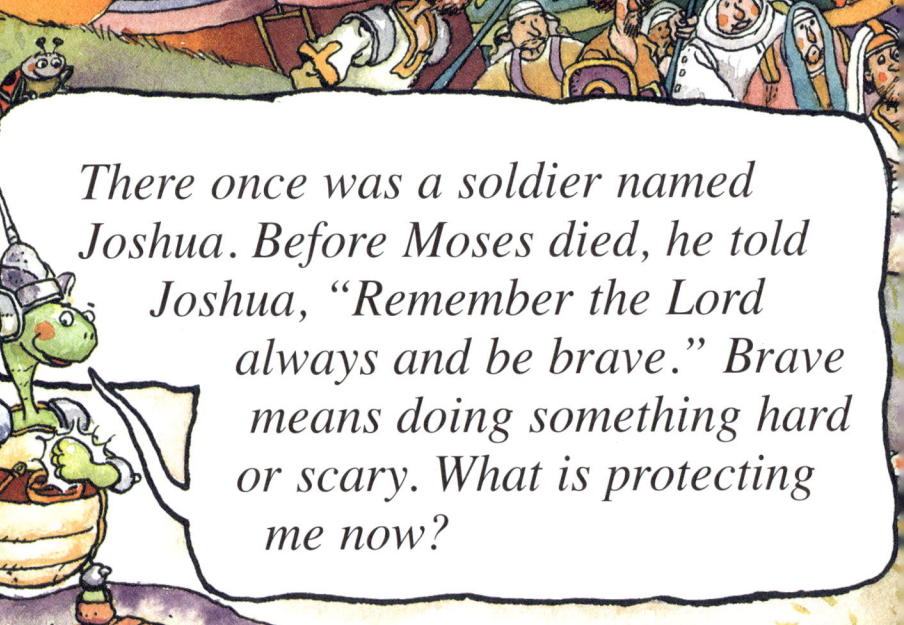

General Joshua and the Promised Land

Joshua 1–2, 5–6; Deuteronomy 31–34

There once was a soldier named Joshua. Before Moses died, he told Joshua, "Remember the Lord always and be brave." Brave means doing something hard or scary. What is protecting me now?

149

God promised Joshua, "I am with you wherever you go. I will help you win the battles for the Promised Land." The first city Joshua had to take was Jericho.

God knew He was asking Joshua to do something hard. That's why he had to be brave. What did you try today that was hard? Did you feel brave?

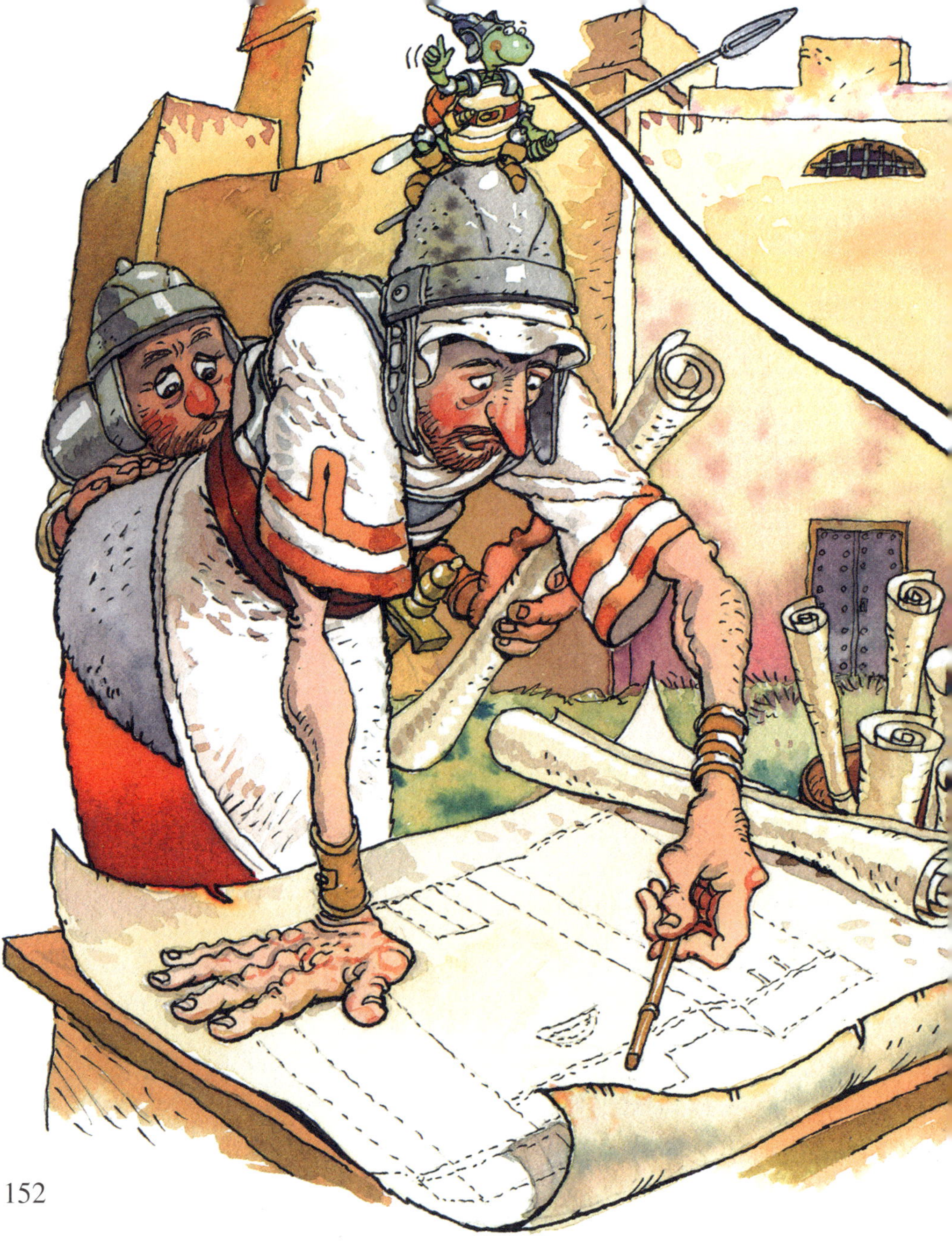

Jericho was shut tight because the people were so afraid. No way in and no way out. The Lord said to Joshua, "Jericho is already yours. This is what you need to do…"

God had a plan. He wanted His people to learn to trust only Him. Name someone you trust.

Make a sound like a trumpet. Now don't say a word... and no sound either!

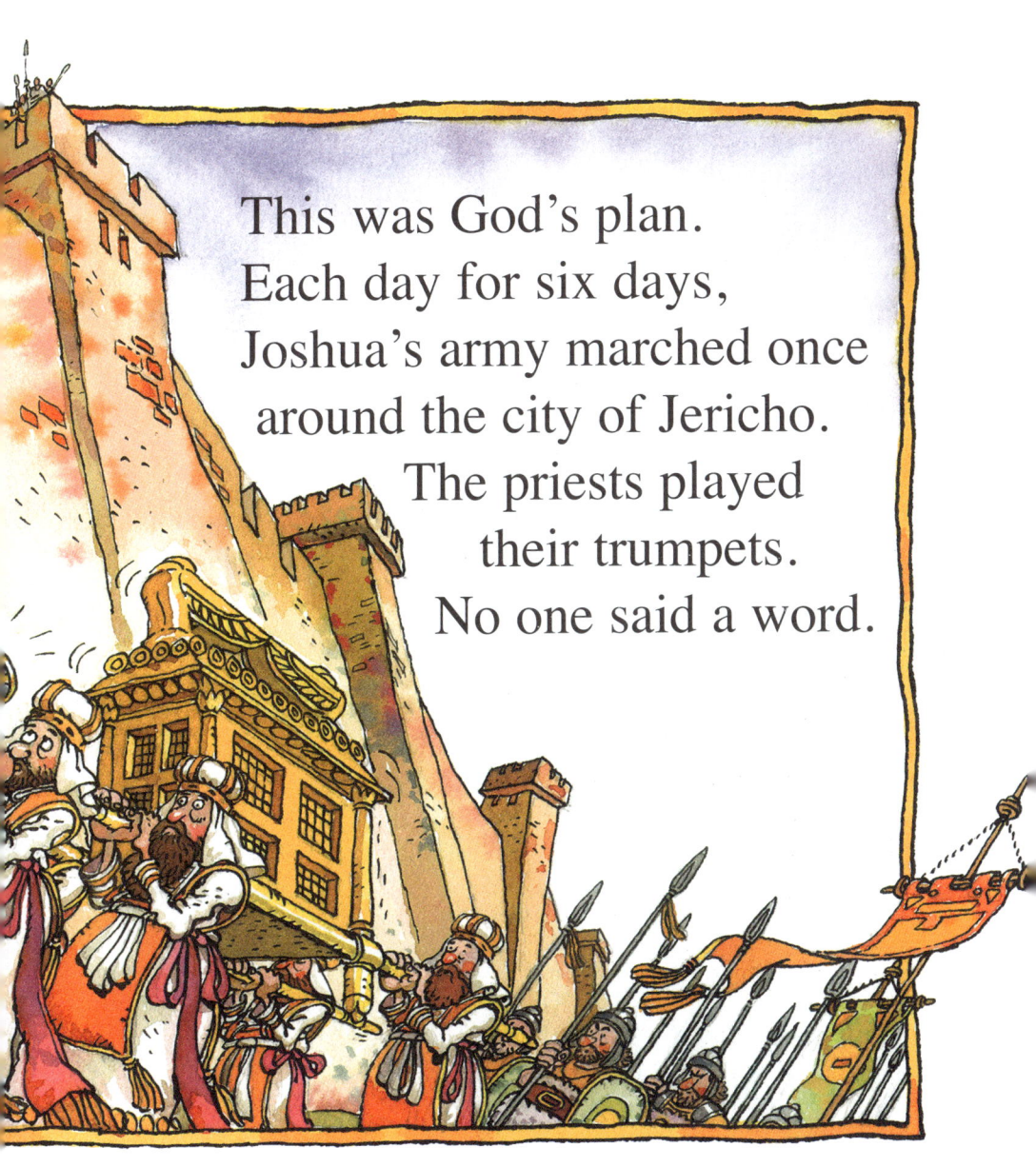

This was God's plan.
Each day for six days,
Joshua's army marched once
around the city of Jericho.
The priests played
their trumpets.
No one said a word.

March around the reader seven times as he or she falls down.

On the seventh day, at dawn, they walked around Jericho seven times. Then, when the priests blew long and hard on their trumpets, Joshua shouted, "Yell! For the Lord has given you Jericho!"

Down tumbled the wall of Jericho! The Lord protected Joshua's people, the Israelites. He made Joshua brave because Joshua remembered the Lord.

God's protection is like a shield, or armor, that we have on all the time, but only notice sometimes—like my shell! Just like Joshua, remember the Lord is with you wherever you go.

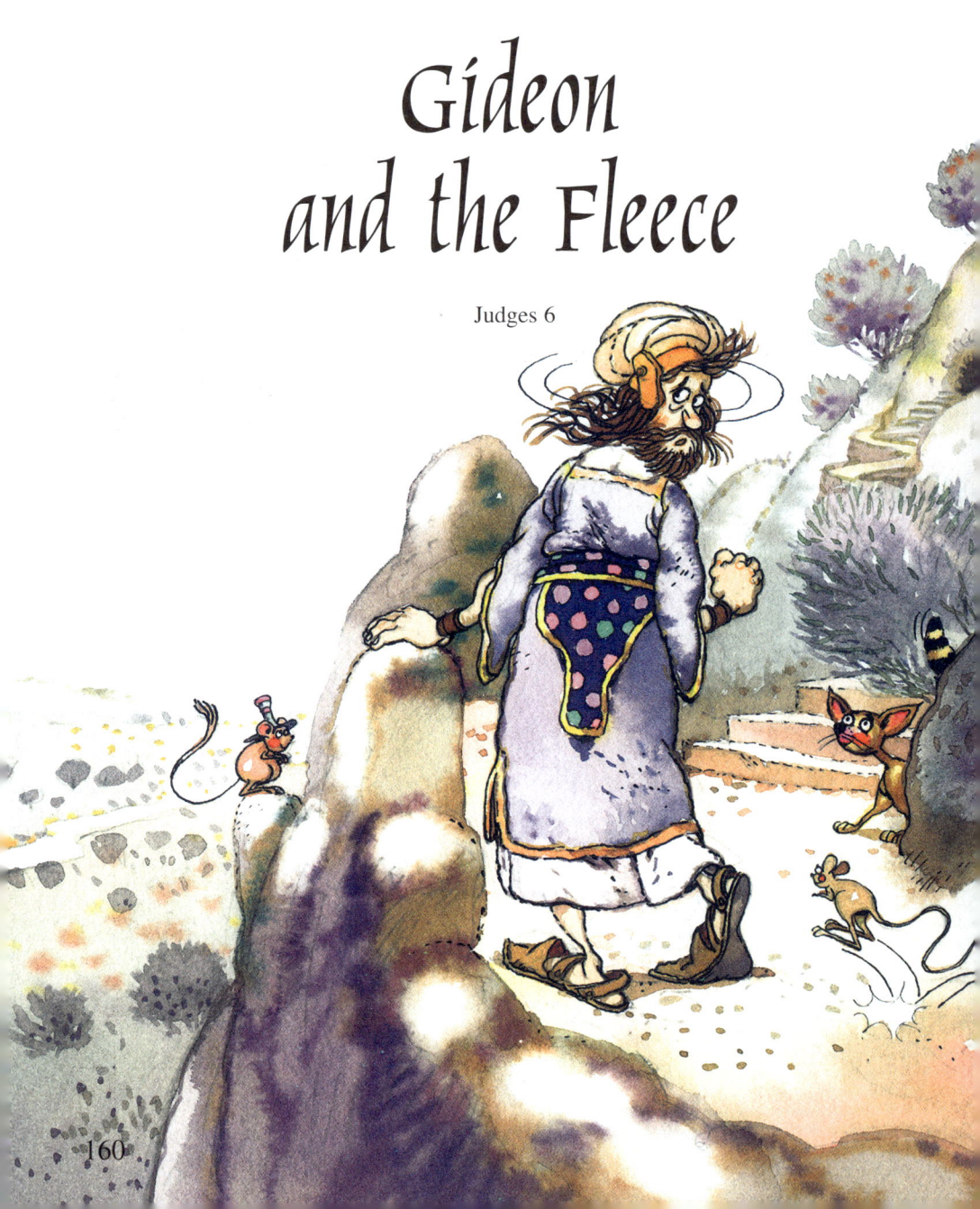

Gideon and the Fleece

Judges 6

There once was a man named Gideon. He was not sure about many things.

God's chosen people, the Israelites, were so scared of the terrible Midianite robbers, they had to hide in caves.

I'm not sure where I am.
I'm not sure where it's safe.
I'm not sure of anything!

The Midianites burned the Israelites' crops and stole their animals. They rode more camels than could be counted.

Can you count how many camels there are? I'm not sure.

165

Gideon had to hide his food from the Midianites. An angel appeared to Gideon and said, "The Lord is with you."

This was something Gideon could be sure of. Say out loud, "The Lord is with me." You can be sure of it!

Then the angel said, "You will lead God's people against the Midianites."

The angel was sure.
But Gideon wasn't so sure.
What do you think?
Are you sure?

Gideon was STILL not sure that God would help the Israelites defeat their enemies. So first he prayed for a wet fleece (or sheepskin) on dry ground.

God did this. Then Gideon prayed for a DRY sheepskin while the ground was wet with dew. God did this, too. NOW Gideon was sure.

171

God had a plan. Gideon and only 300 soldiers surrounded the enemy camp and made a tremendous noise!

They held the torches in their left hands and the trumpets in their right hands, and won the battle!

Raise your left hand. Raise your right hand. Hooray for Gideon! Hooray for God!

Samson the Super Strong

Judges 13–14, 16

When Samson was a little boy, he was very special.

174

175

God asked Samson's parents to never cut his hair. This was a sign that God had a special plan for Samson. As Samson got older, and his hair grew and grew, he became very strong.

Let's see your muscles. How strong are you?

One day Samson used
God's gift of super strength
when he was attacked. By what?
He threw off and killed a great,
big, ferocious, ROARING. . .

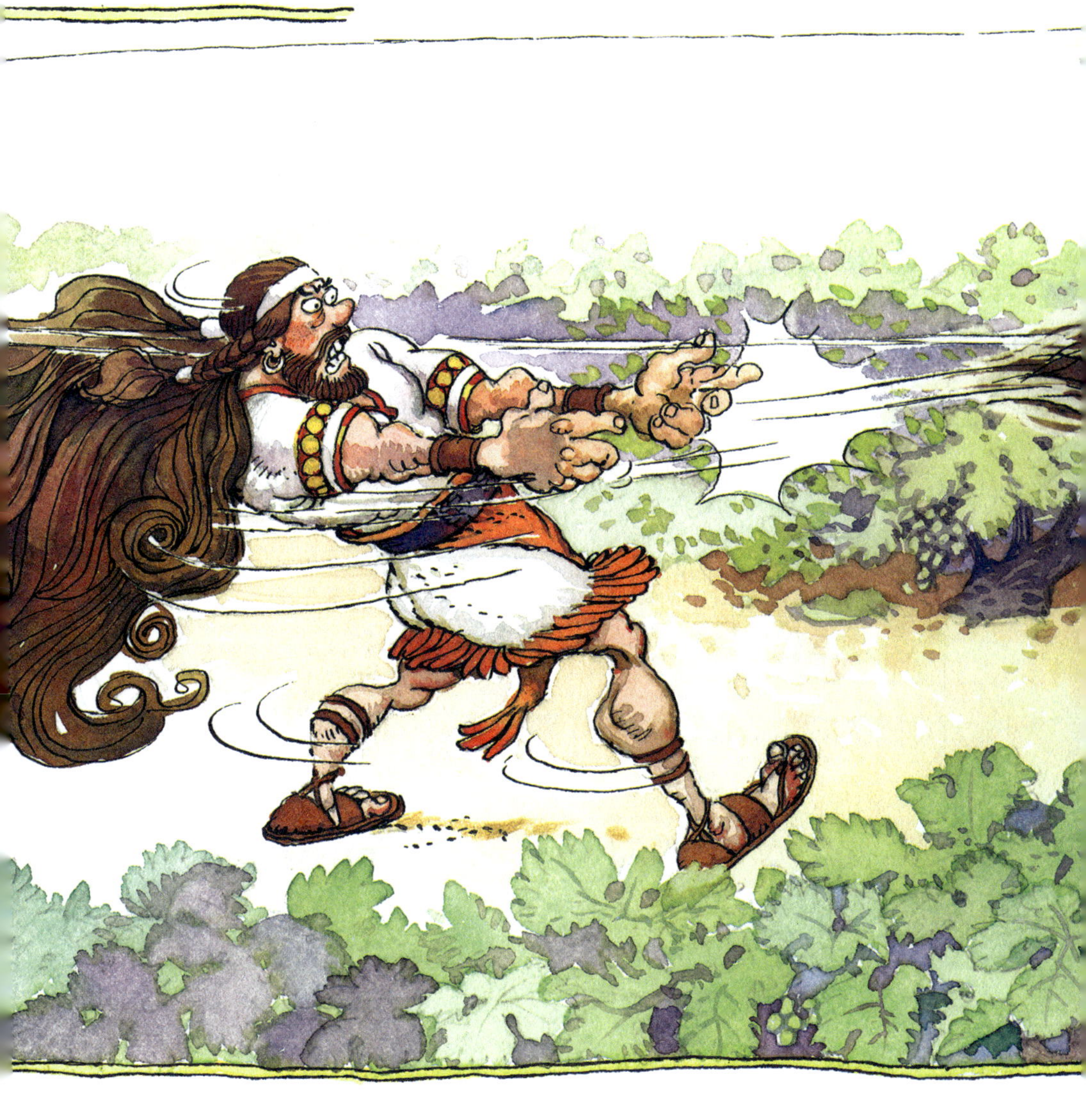

...LION!! How strong is a lion? Was he stronger than Samson? Stronger than you? How big is a lion?

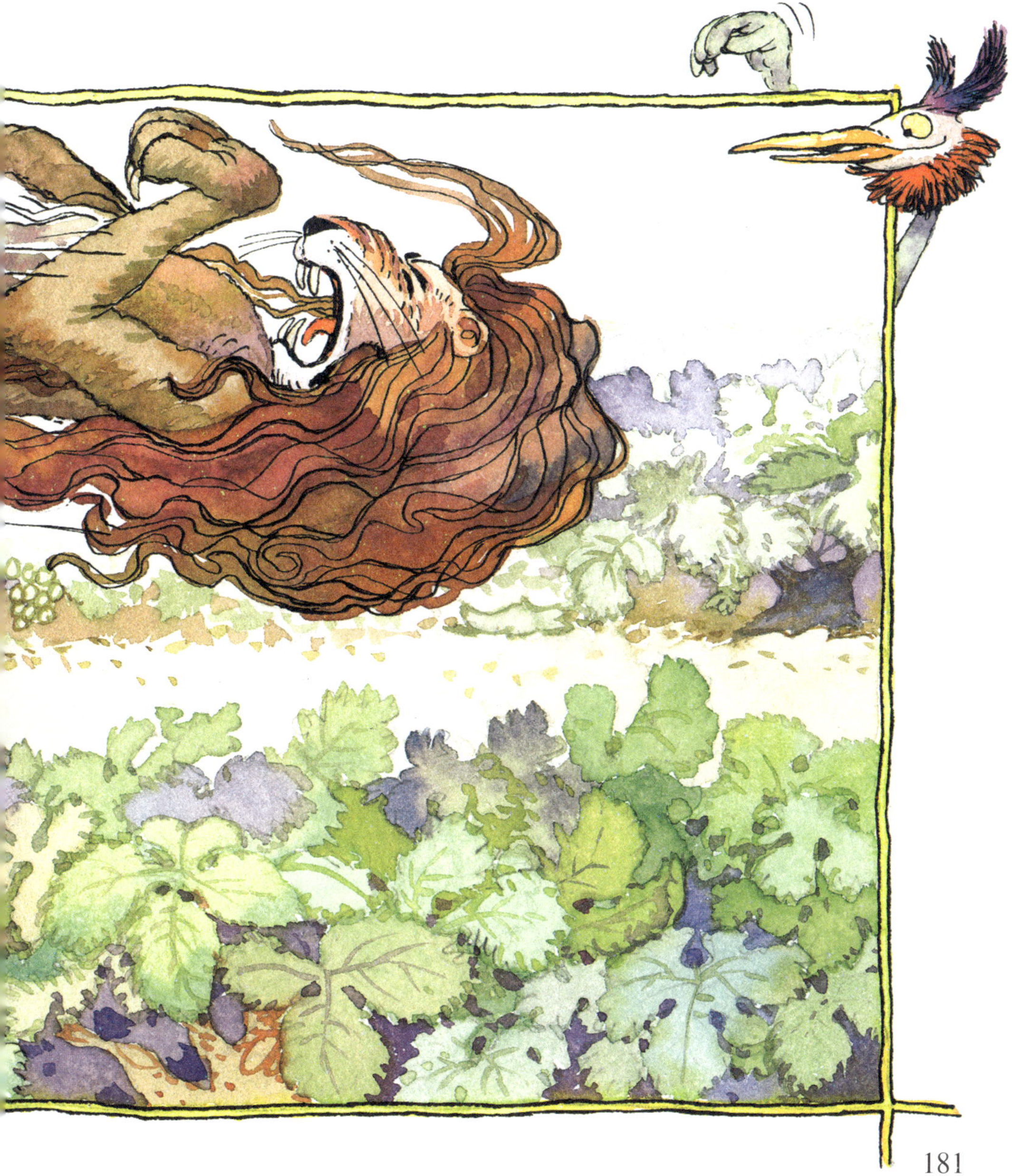

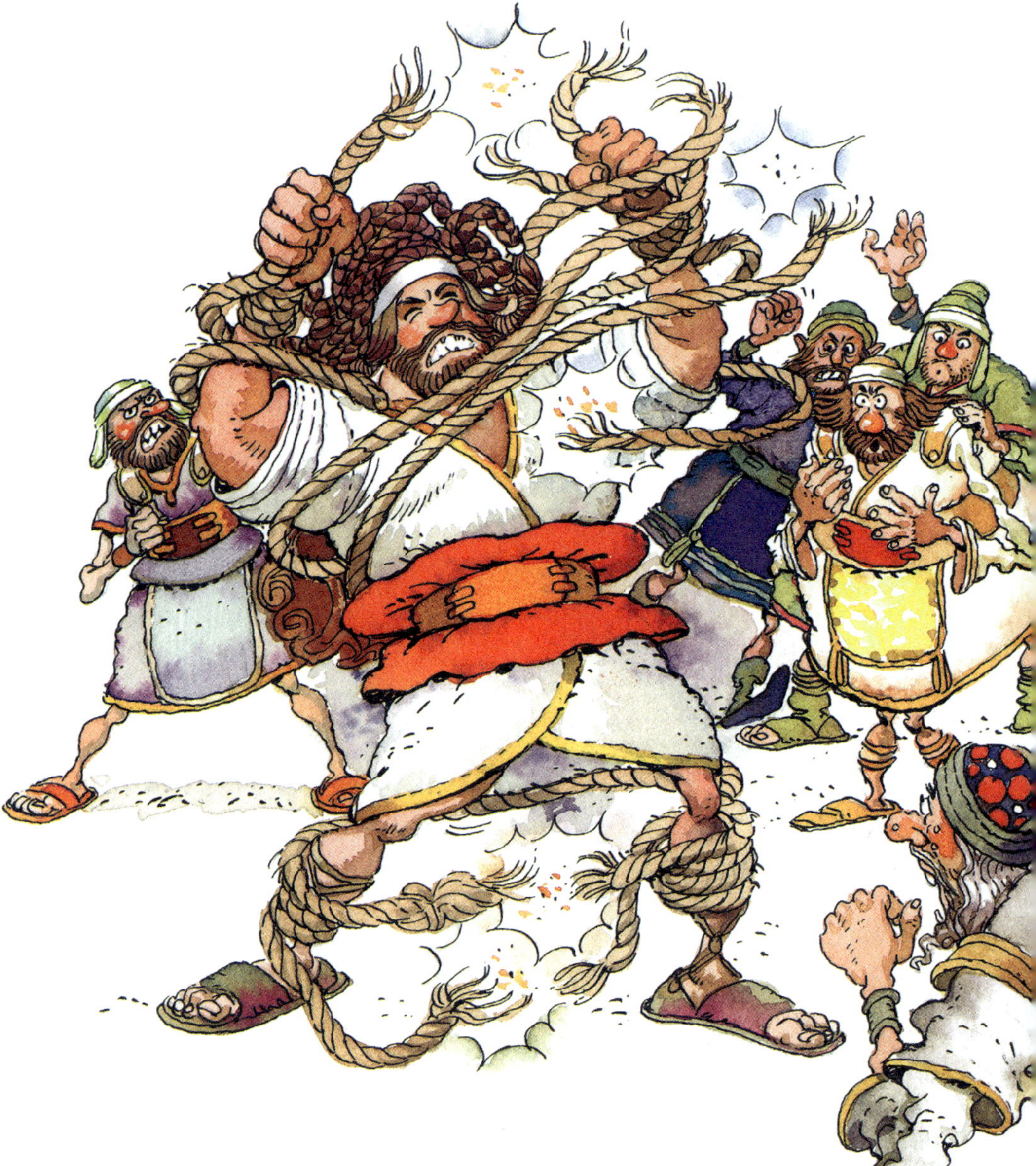

Another time, Samson's enemies took him prisoner and tied him up. Again, the Spirit of the Lord made him super strong, and he broke the ropes as if they were nothing but thread!

You try to break a thread. Now try to break two!

Years later, Samson fell in love with a woman named Delilah. She nagged and begged Samson to tell her the secret of his strength. Samson's secret was that his hair had never been cut.

Samson's enemies promised to pay Delilah money if she tricked Samson. When he told her his secret, she told his enemies. They jumped Samson and cut his hair.

Oh no! Samson wasn't super strong anymore!

Samson's enemies put him in jail and hurt his eyes so he could not see. Samson prayed and as his hair grew long again, Samson grew stronger. Then he pushed down the palace walls, destroying all his enemies.
CRASH!

What makes YOU different? Your fingers, your toes? Let's see. God has a special plan for your life, different from Samson's, but just as special!

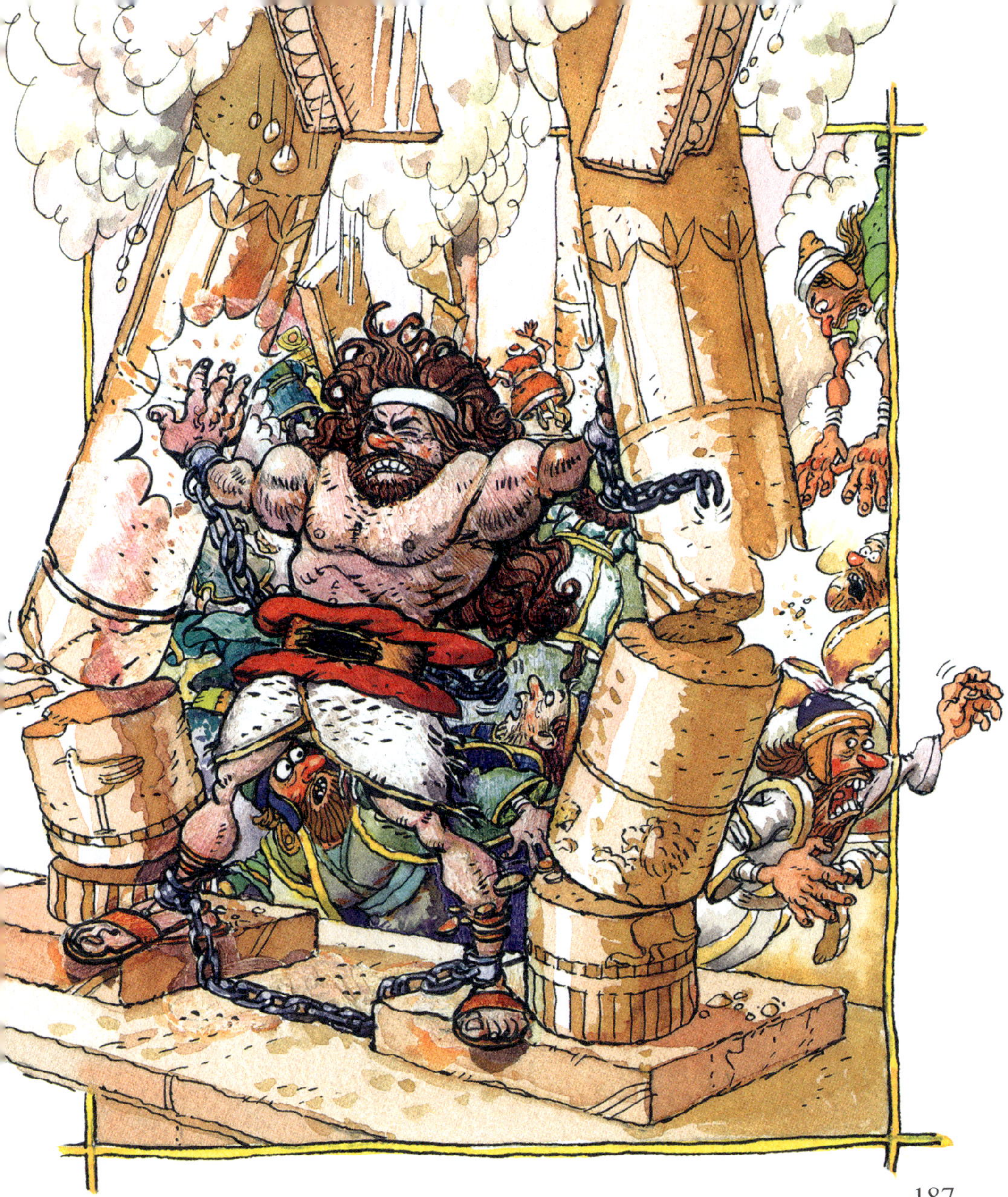

Ruth Must Find a New Home

Ruth 1–2

There once was a young woman named Ruth. She married a man from another country and loved him very much.

Then Ruth's husband died. His mother, Naomi, told Ruth, "You should go back home to your own parents." Naomi wanted to return to her home, and to God's people in Israel.

In what country were you born? Is that the same country you live in now?

Ruth was very special because she loved God. And she loved Naomi, who had taught her to love God.

Who has taught you to love God?

Ruth begged Naomi, "Please let me go with you. I will go where you go. Your people will be my people and your God, my God. He will take care of us."

Point to things that are the same color as the colors of your country's flag.

In what city were you born?
Is that your home now?

Naomi and Ruth walked a long, long way. They walked all the way to Bethlehem, the city where Naomi was born, their new home!

God Rewards Ruth's Loyalty

Ruth 2-4

In Bethlehem, Ruth took care of Naomi. She gathered leftover grain and shared it with Naomi.

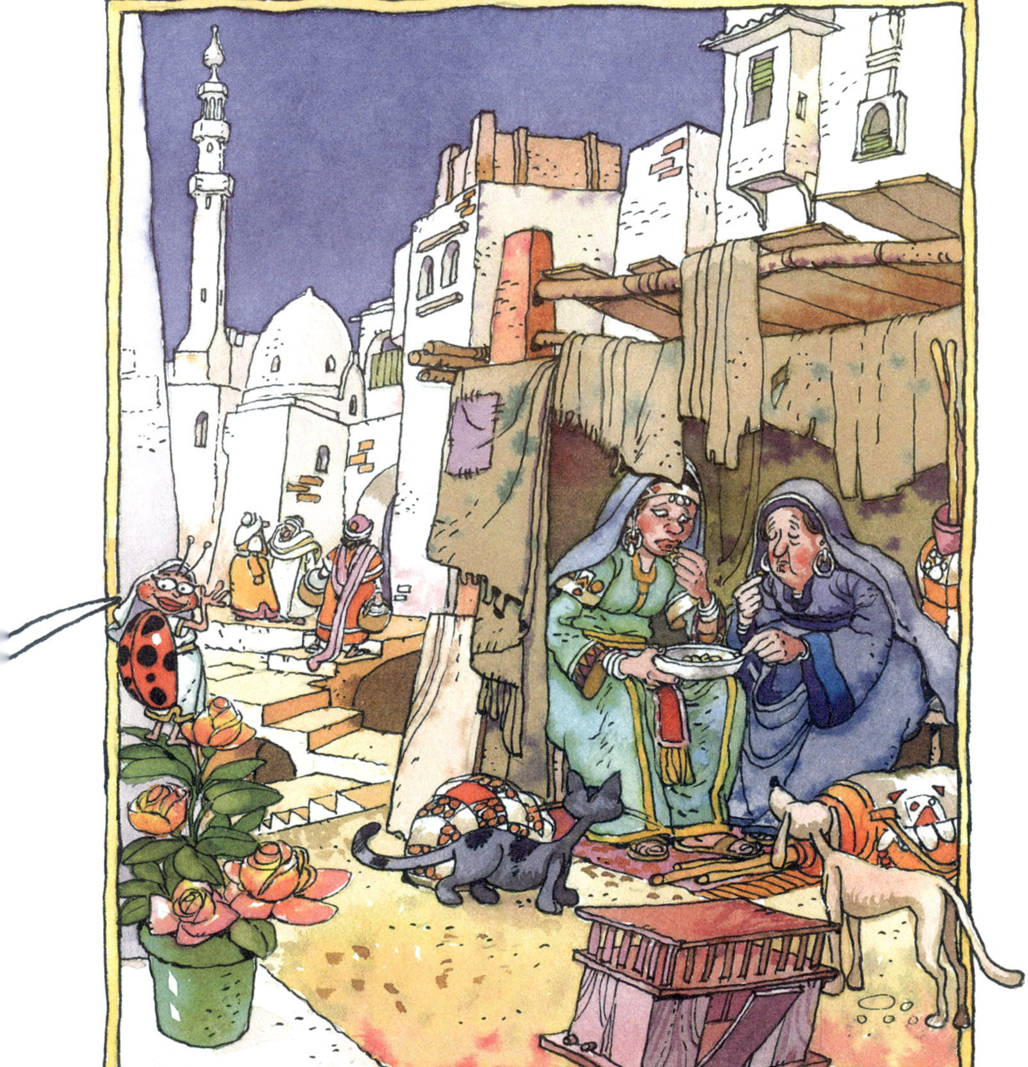

The field where Ruth found food belonged to a man named Boaz. Boaz wanted to help Ruth because she wanted to help Naomi.

Boaz let Ruth take home as much grain as she wanted. Naomi said, "Does Boaz own the field? He is a relative of mine!"

Naomi told Ruth, "Because Boaz is from my family and cares about us, maybe he will marry you."

Your family cares for you. God cares for your family. Whom do you care for?

Ruth and Boaz were married and there was a big party. Naomi was very, very happy!

Who loves you? Does that make you happy? Show how happy you are by smiling the biggest smile in the world!

Now Ruth and Boaz could take care of Naomi together. After a while, they had a little baby boy called Obed. Naomi was like a grandmother to Obed.

Does someone who loves you have a special name for you?

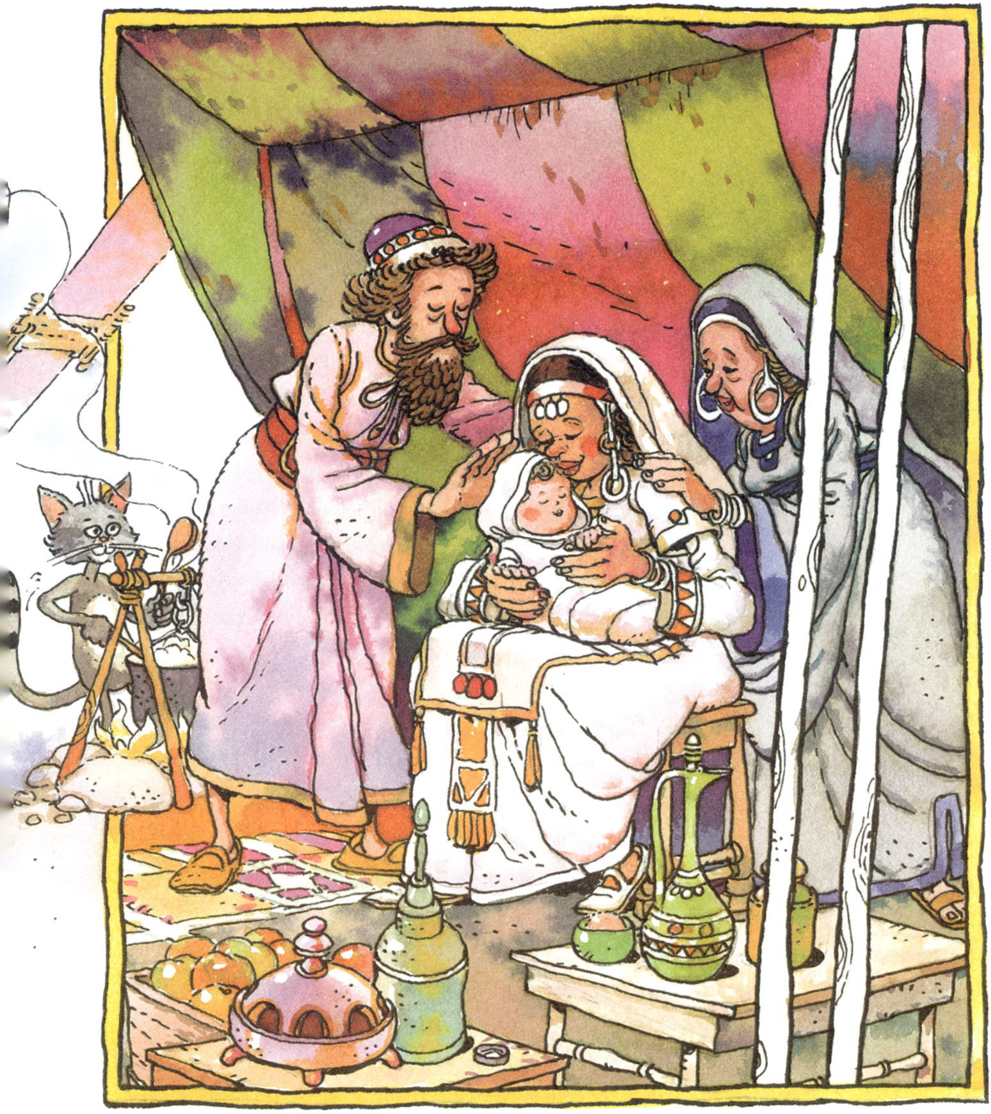

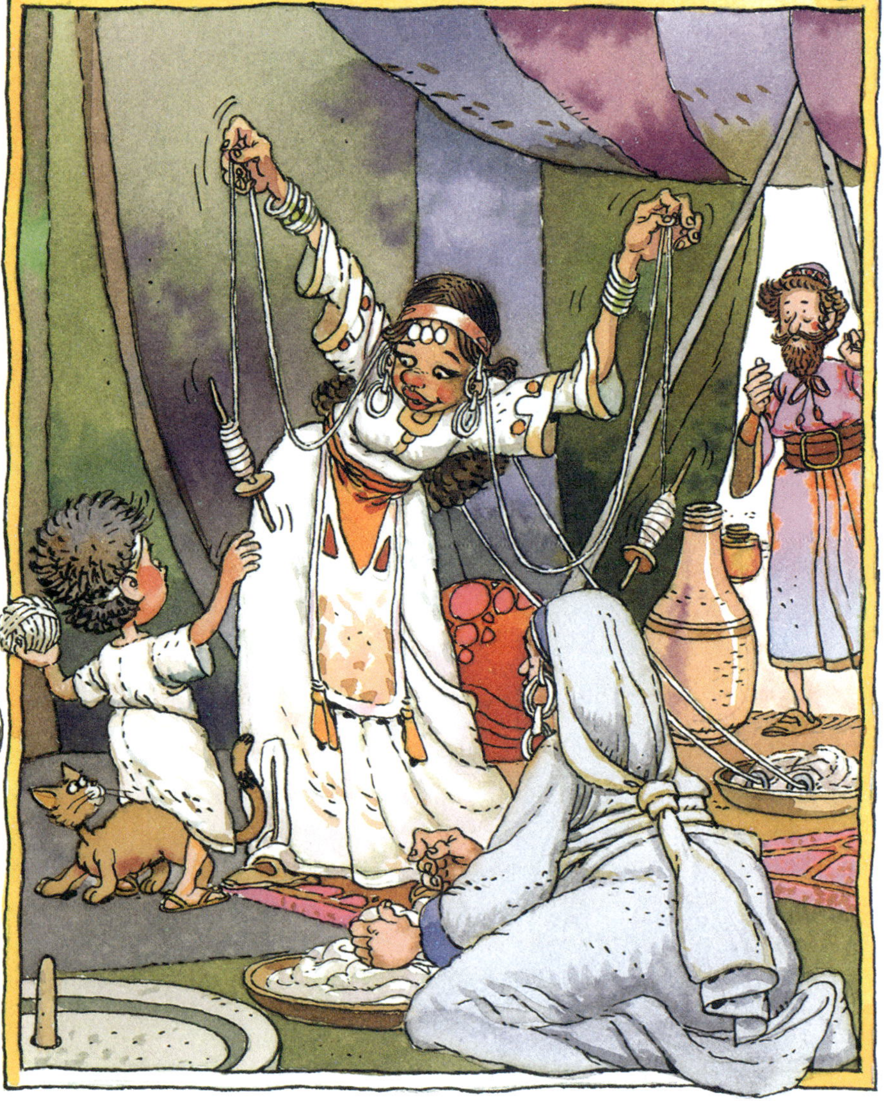

Ruth had been a stranger when she came to Bethlehem. But God blessed her because she did what He wanted her to do.

Ruth had left her own people and country out of loyalty and kindness to Naomi. She started with nothing, and now had a husband and son and a new home in Bethlehem!

Many, many years later, King David was born in Bethlehem. Many, many years after that, Jesus was born in Bethlehem. And they were both part of the same family, with Obed as a great-great-great-grandfather, and Ruth as his mother.

Who was your great-great-great-grandfather? And who was his mother? Thank God now for your family and your home.

God Chooses David

1 Samuel 16

God looked at the heart of a shepherd boy named David and saw David loved Him very much.

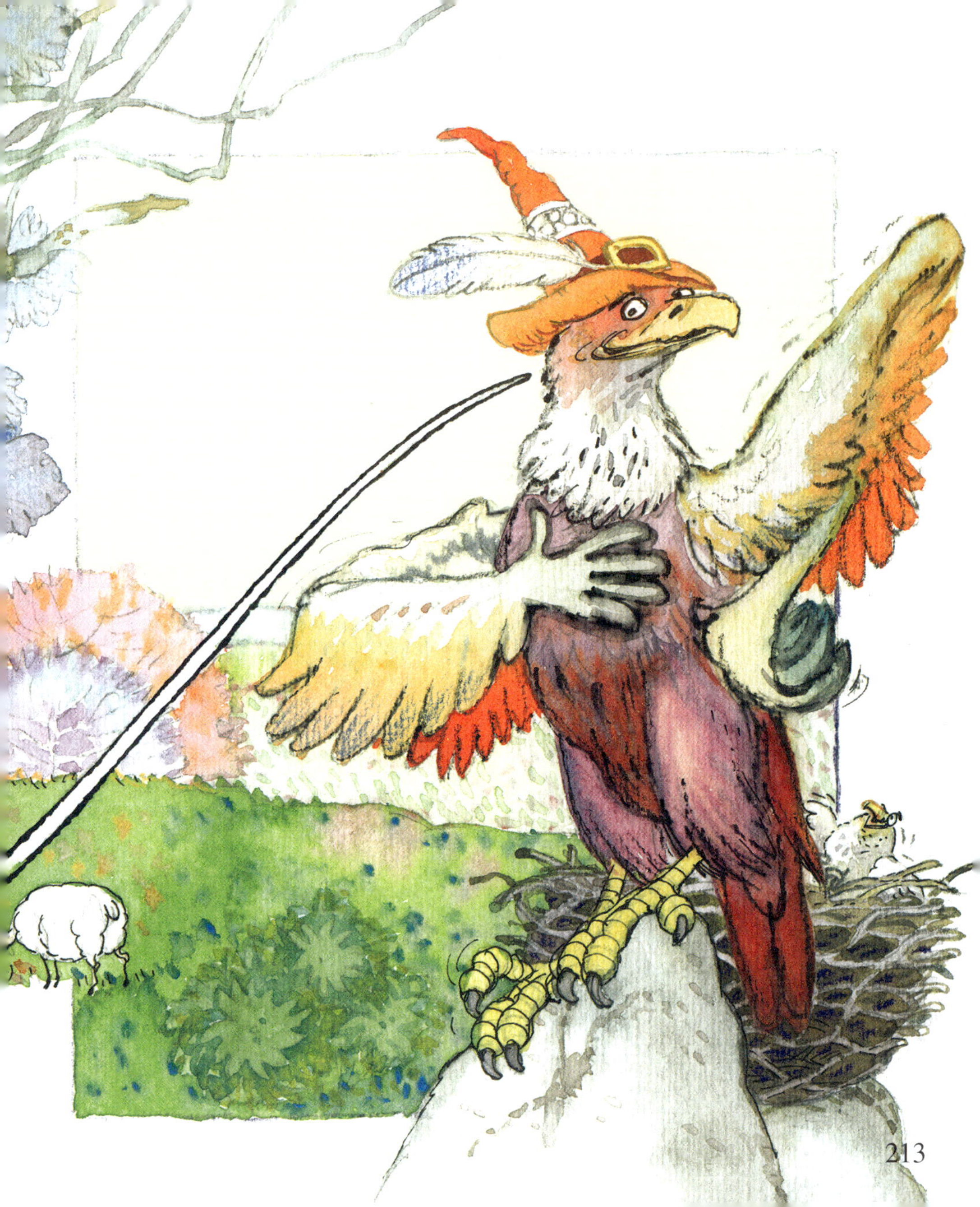

David liked to play his harp
and sing songs for God.

Can you look at your heart? Can you feel it? Do you feel good when you do good?

Name one thing you are good at.

David was also very good at slinging stones. He could hit whatever he aimed at. He could even kill bears that hunted his sheep.

He could EVEN kill lions with his sling!

Can you roar as loud as a lion?

A wise man named Samuel came to David's family to find God's choice for king. Not this brother, not this one, not this one, not this one, not this one, not this one, not this one!

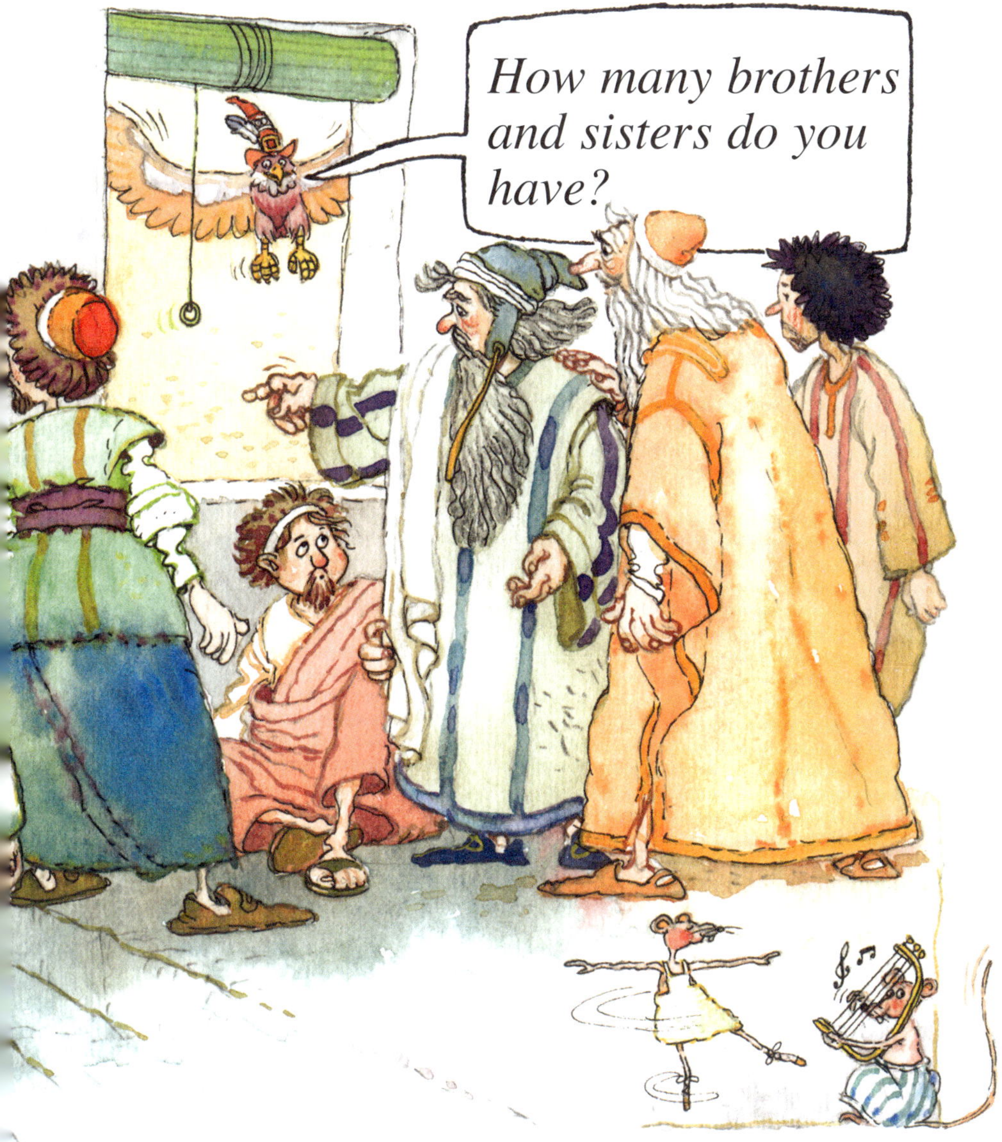
How many brothers and sisters do you have?

"Are these seven boys all of your sons?" Samuel asked.

"No," David's father answered. "I have one more. The youngest."

God chose David because God had plans for David. Not now, but someday David would become king.

"Sometimes being the youngest isn't so bad."

David Fights Goliath

1 Samuel 17

Sometimes it's scary being small.

The army of Israel was mighty and great in number. Still, the soldiers were very, VERY scared of fighting the giant GOLIATH!

What is a bully?

227

No one in the army dared to fight Goliath. David was too small to be in the army like his brothers, but he still begged King Saul, "Let me fight Goliath! I'm good with a sling."

David knew God was on his side.

The giant named Goliath was making fun of God and God's people. "You're nothing, and so is your God!" This was a terrible thing to say. David said, "Oh, yeah? You're not too big for me!"

Has anyone ever made fun of you because you're the smallest or youngest?

David took aim at the giant and sent a stone whistling through the air with his sling. The stone flew and flew until . . . "PING!" It hit Goliath in the head and killed him!

> *It's not always the big and strong who win. Sometimes it's the small and brave.*

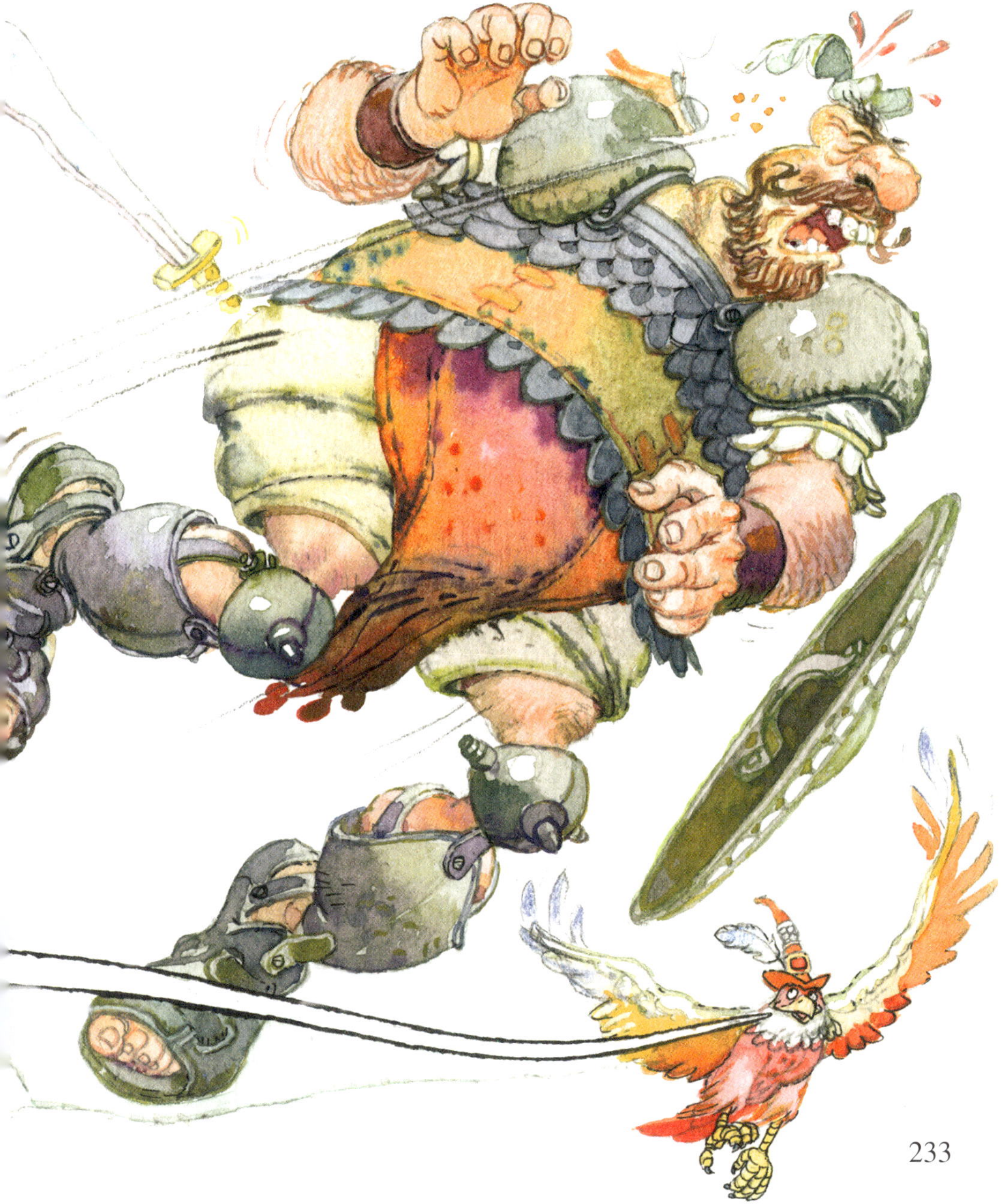

After David killed Goliath, everyone said, "Three cheers for young David! Hip, hip hooray! Young David is brave and handsome."

Was David special because he was smart and brave and handsome and good? No. Because God chose him and loved him. Just like God loves YOU!

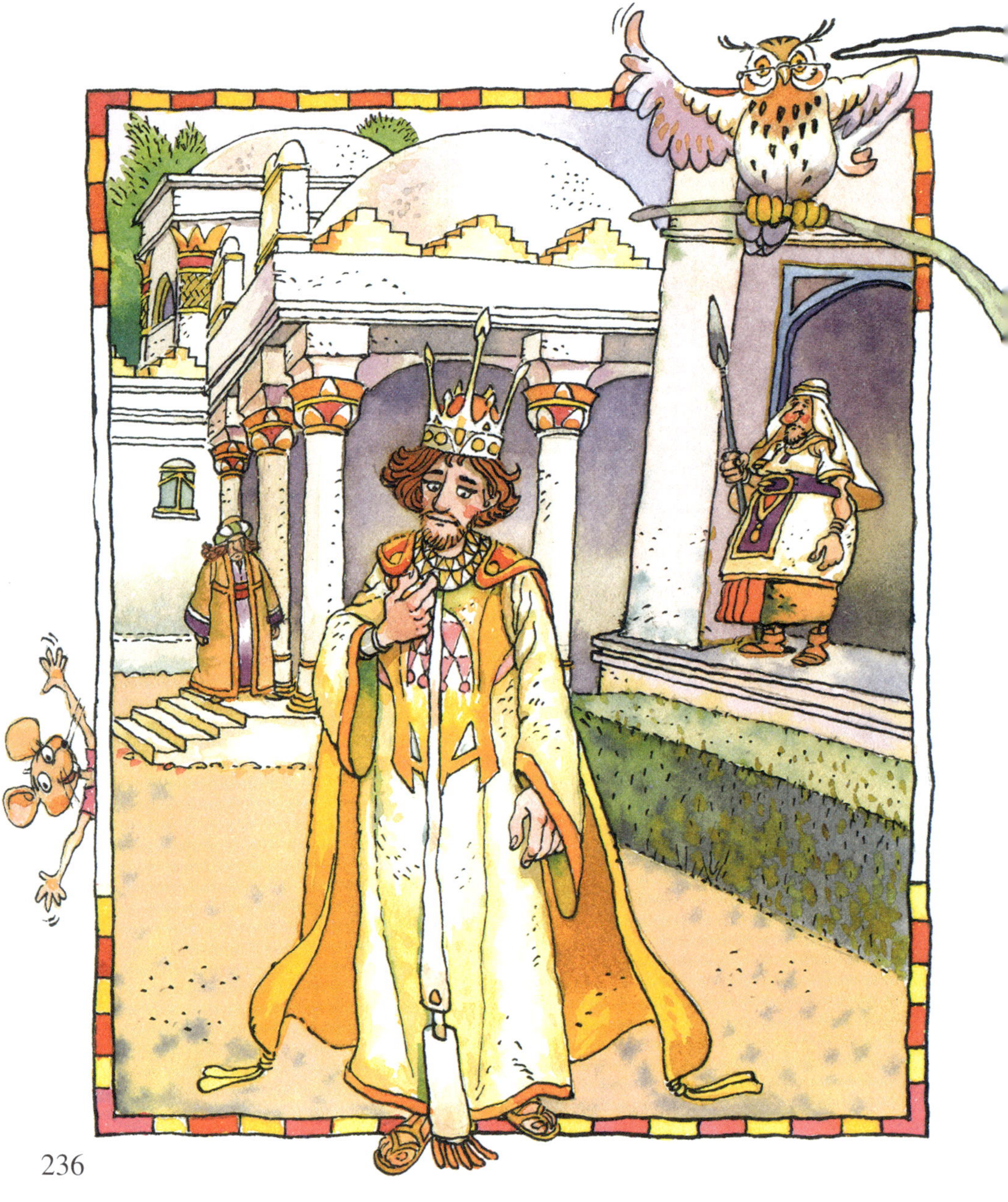

Solomon Saves a Baby

2 Samuel 12; 1 Kings 3; 2 Chronicles 1

When Solomon was a young prince, God said in a dream, "Make a wish for whatever you want."
Solomon said, "Please give me wisdom. Help me see what is right and wrong. I want to rule Your people wisely."

If you could wish for anything in the whole wide world, what would you wish for?

God granted Solomon's wish for wisdom. People came from all over to ask his advice, including two mothers who were fighting over a little baby.

"He's mine!" shouted one mother.
"No, he's mine!" shouted the other.

Who do YOU think the real mother is?

Solomon needed to find out which woman was the baby's mother. When he said, "Cut the baby in half," the people gasped. Solomon wasn't going to hurt the baby. He was finding out the truth.

If this is too scary, make a gasping sound as loud as you can.

The first woman cried, "No! Please, give the baby to her. Then at least he will live."

Solomon pointed at the first woman. "Give the baby to her. She is the real mother because she cared more for the baby's life than for her own wishes."

Wisdom is being smart and having common sense, knowing what you're doing and why.

Go find something you used to fight over, but won't anymore.

The Wisdom of King Solomon

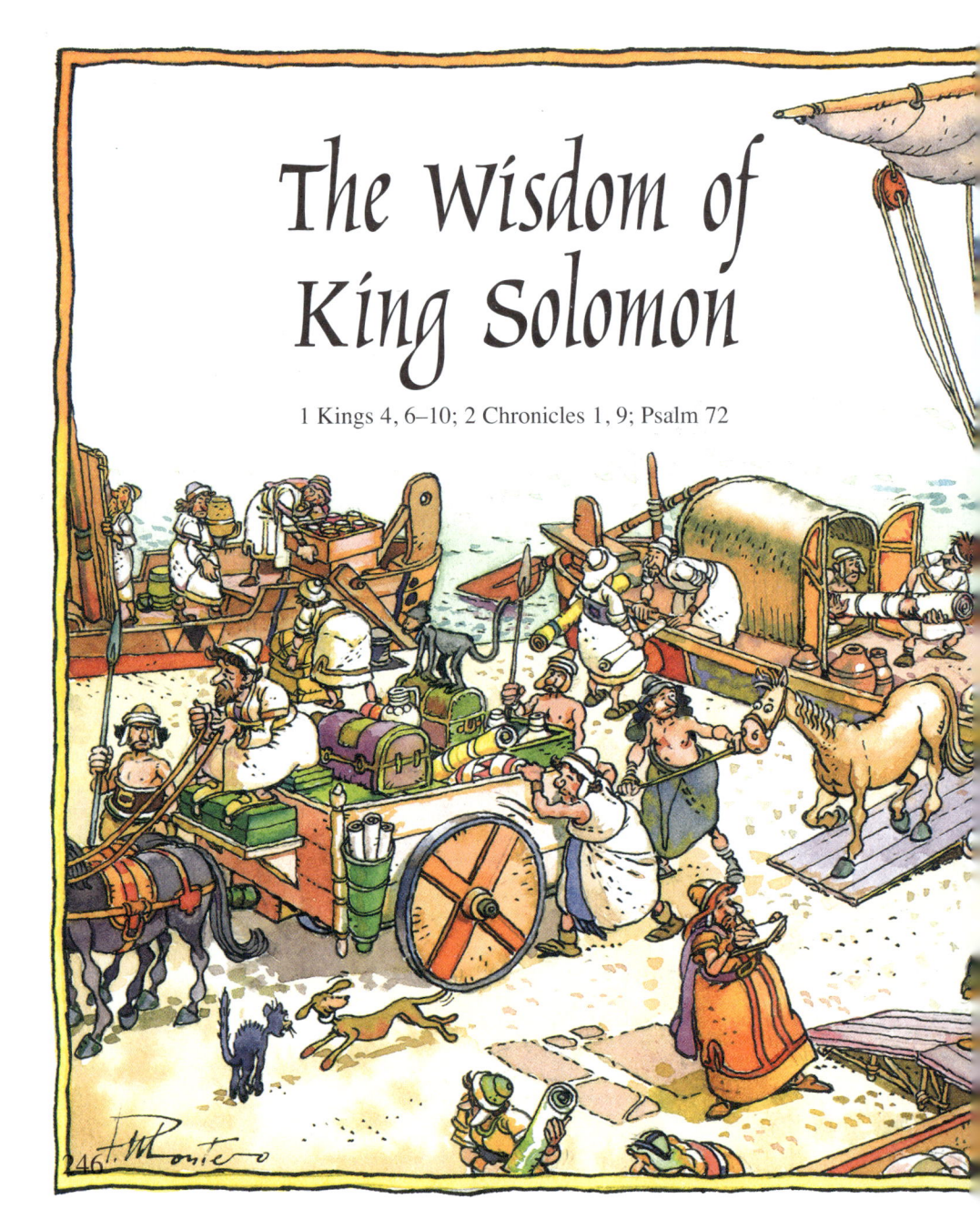

1 Kings 4, 6–10; 2 Chronicles 1, 9; Psalm 72

Because of his wisdom, Solomon had power. He had armies, and a fleet of ships that traded in gold, silver, ivory, and horses. Can you make horse noises?

Solomon had palaces for himself. But he also built a great big house for God. This was the temple, a place to put the Ten Commandments God wrote for Moses, a place for God's people to worship Him.

249

Can you take your building blocks and make a church?

Remember your wish? Was it for a big house or a bigger room of your own?

Solomon was so wise, the Queen of Sheba visited him with gifts of gold and spices.

253

Solomon said children should listen to advice if they want to make their parents proud. Parents show their love for their children by teaching them what is right and what is wrong.

*Remember your wish?
Name one thing money cannot buy.*

Elijah the Prophet

1 Kings 16–17, 19; 2 Kings 2

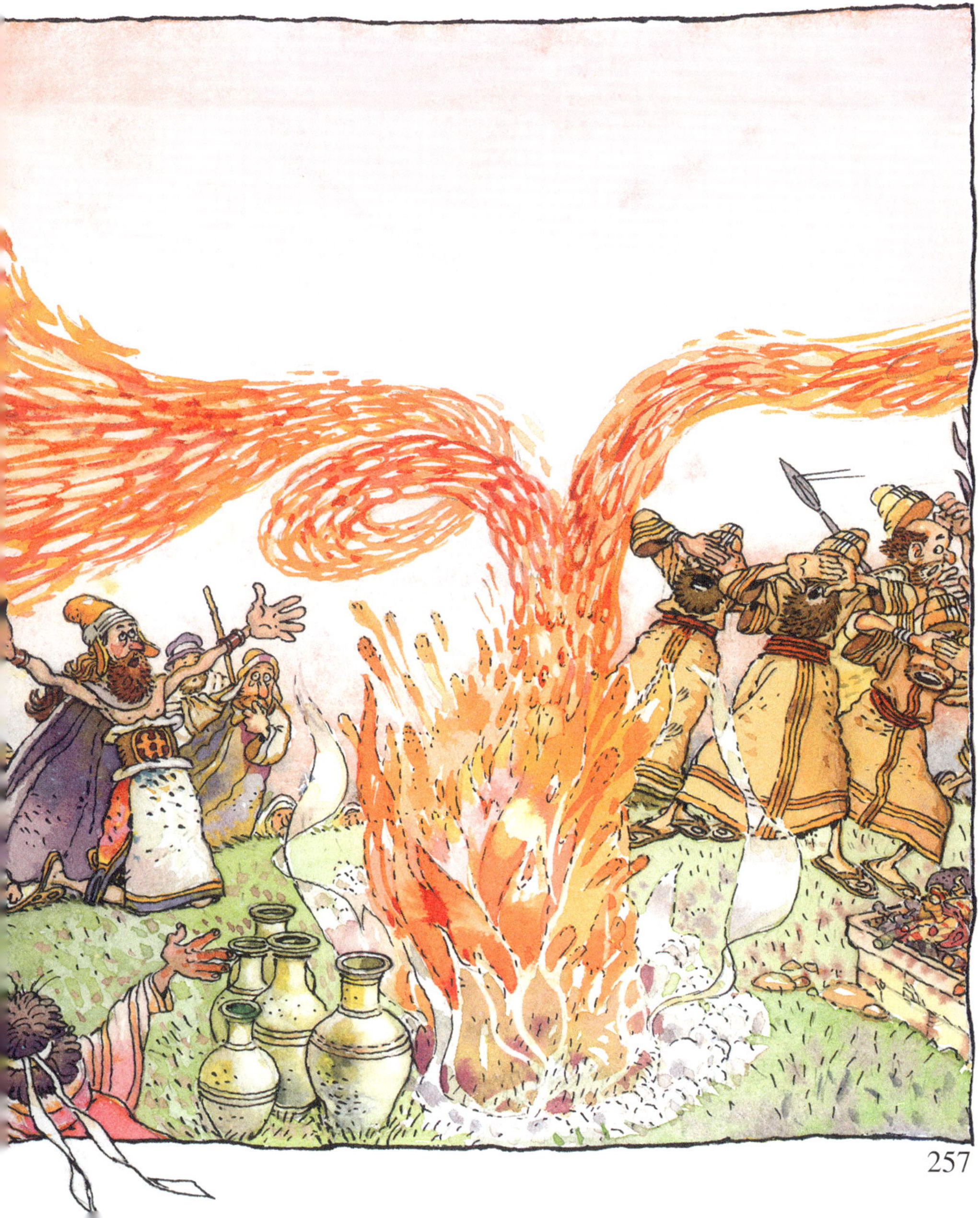

Elijah was a prophet. A prophet is someone who sees, a see-er from God. He sees what is happening now. He sometimes sees what is going to happen. Close your eyes, then open them. Now you can see!

259

Elijah's job was to warn the people, "Turn back to God!" Because he was a prophet, he SAW people in some of the same ways God saw them.

The king and most of the people did not even believe in God. Instead they prayed to false gods. This was a terrible thing! How would YOU warn someone? What would you say?

God sent Elijah to a village to ask a widow and her son for food and water. Although she was very poor, she still gave him their water, then offered her last handful of flour and drops of oil.

The widow had almost nothing, yet she shared it with Elijah. God rewarded her by promising to keep her bowl of flour and jar of oil from going empty. What is something you can eat that has flour and oil in it?

Elijah stayed with the widow and her son three years. But then her son died! Elijah called on God to bring the boy back to life. And God answered his prayer!

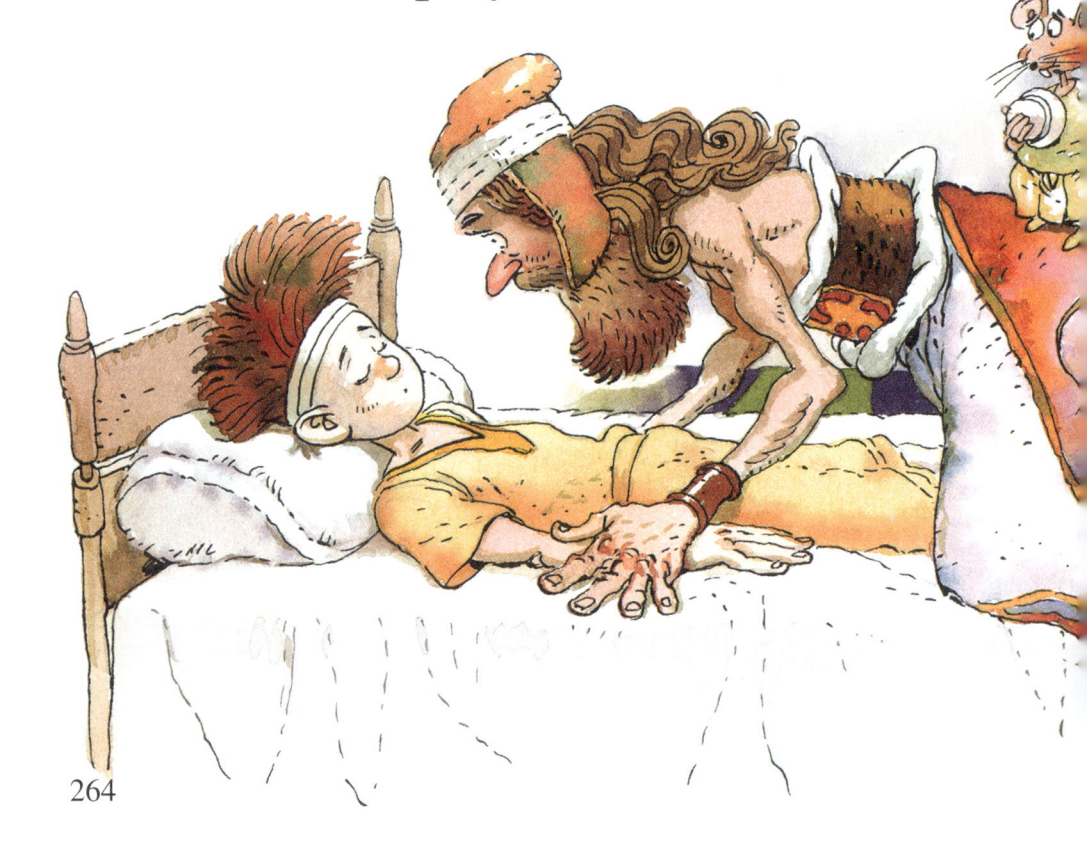

When Elijah took the live son (who had been dead) to the widow, she knew Elijah was a man of God!

One day, Elijah climbed a mountain and the Lord said He would pass by him. But He wasn't in a strong wind. The Lord wasn't in an earthquake, and He wasn't in a fire. Elijah found God in the gentle whispering of the wind.

Move your hands and make a sound like the gentle whispering of the wind.

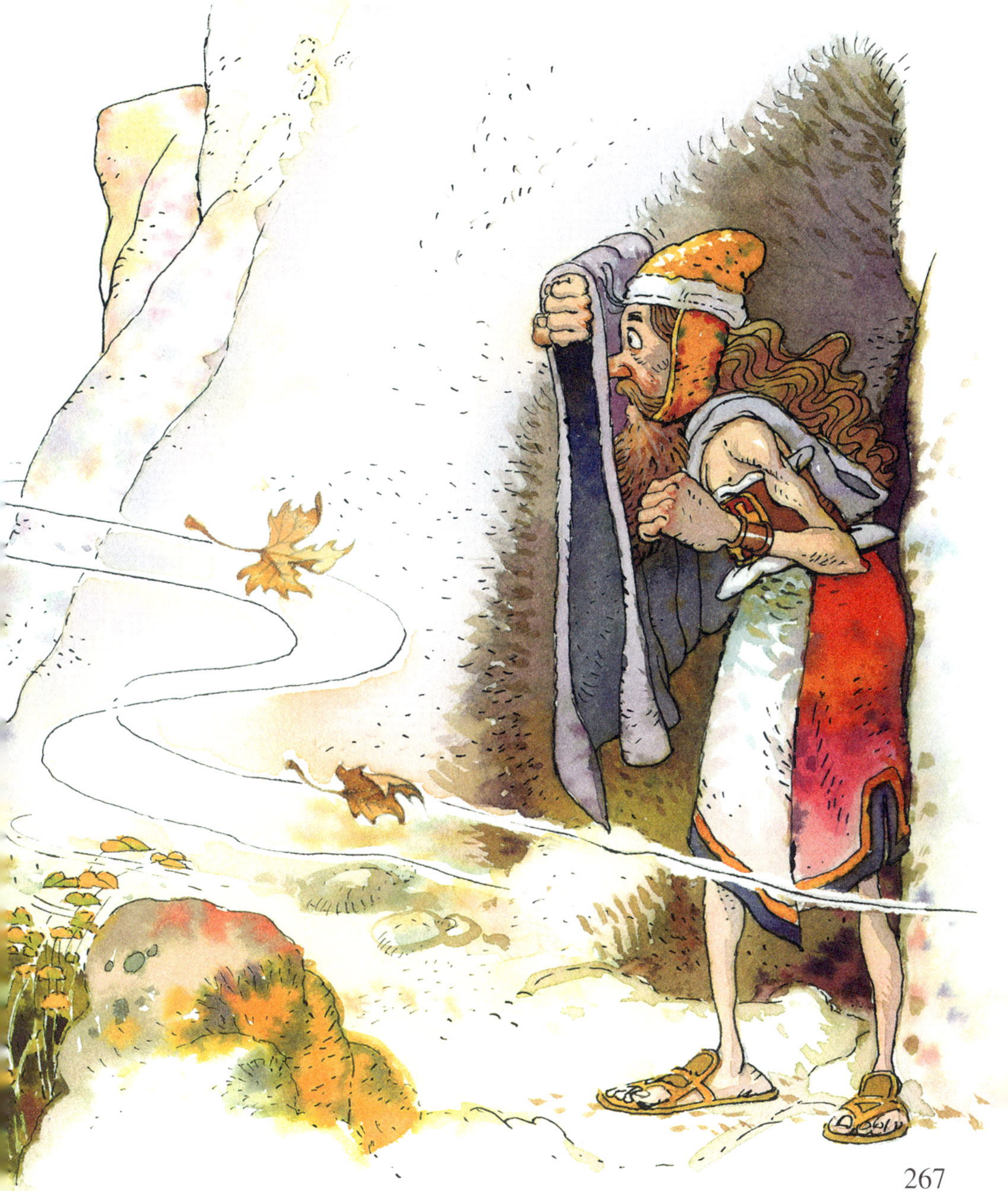

When Elijah was very, very old, God sent horses made of fire galloping through the sky to meet him. Elijah jumped into the chariot of fire they were pulling and went up to heaven.

What a SIGHT that must have been! What sound does a horse make?

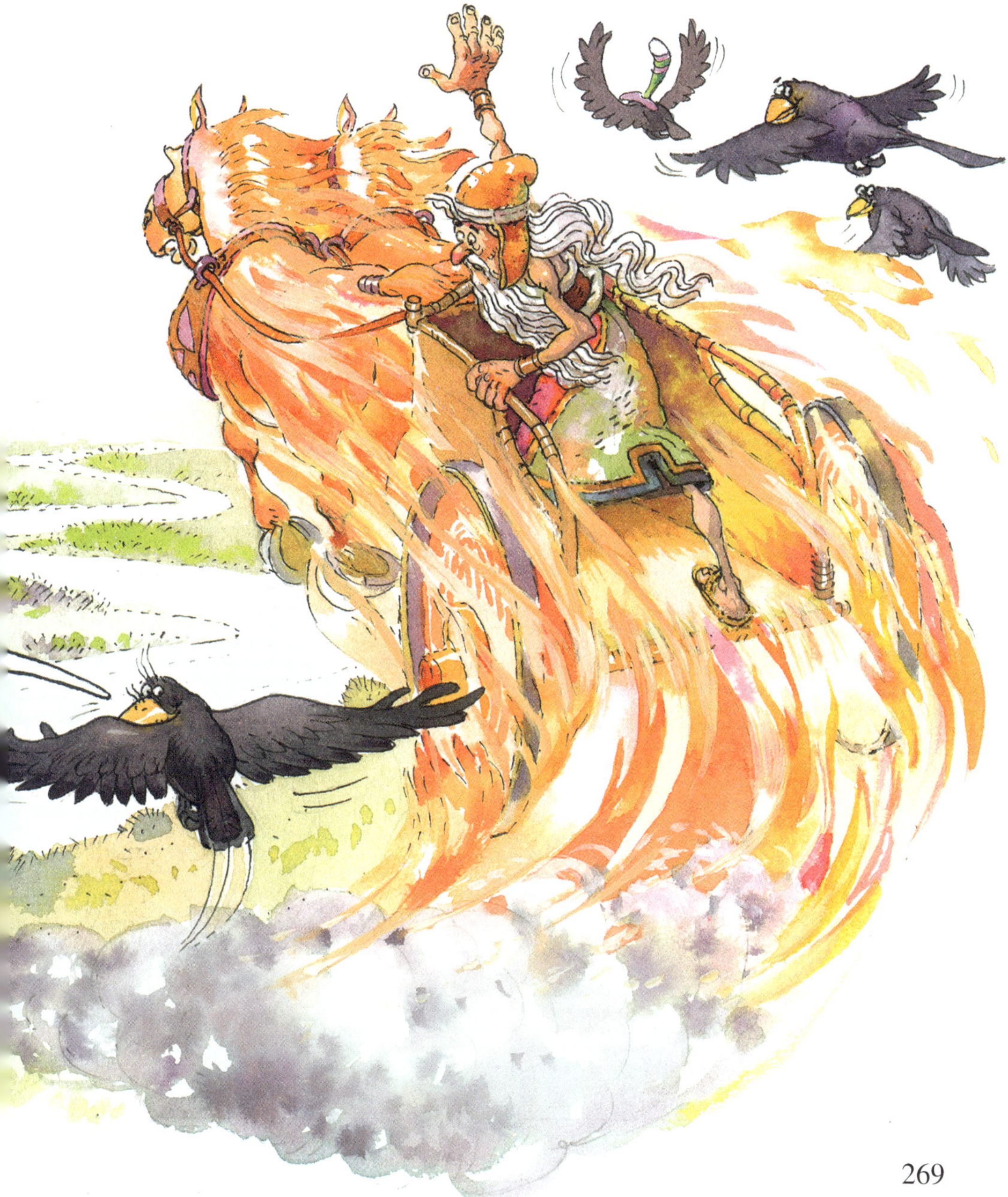

Jonah Tries to Run from God

Jonah 1

There once was a man named Jonah. God told Jonah to go to Nineveh: "Go warn your enemies to change their ways."

271

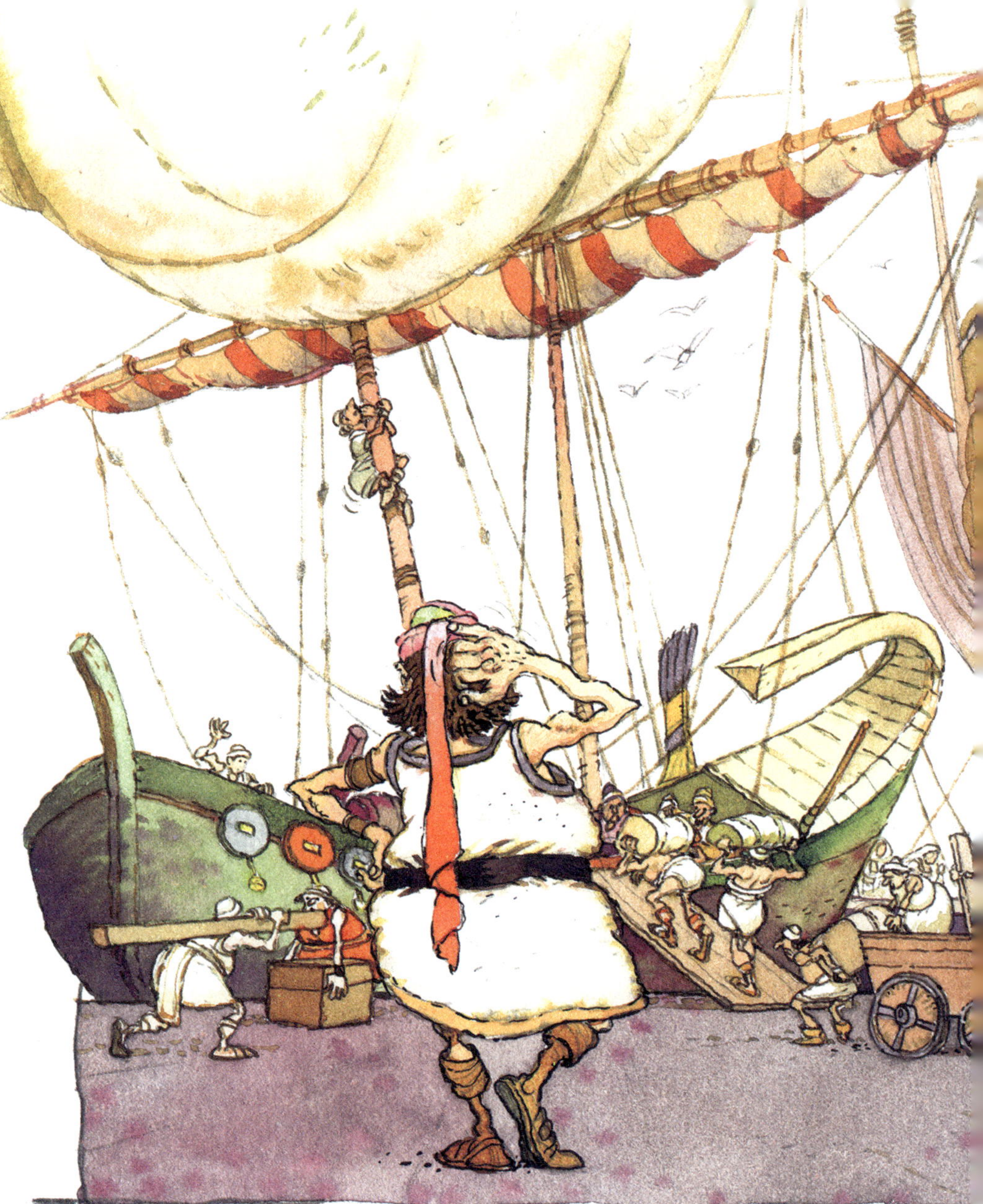

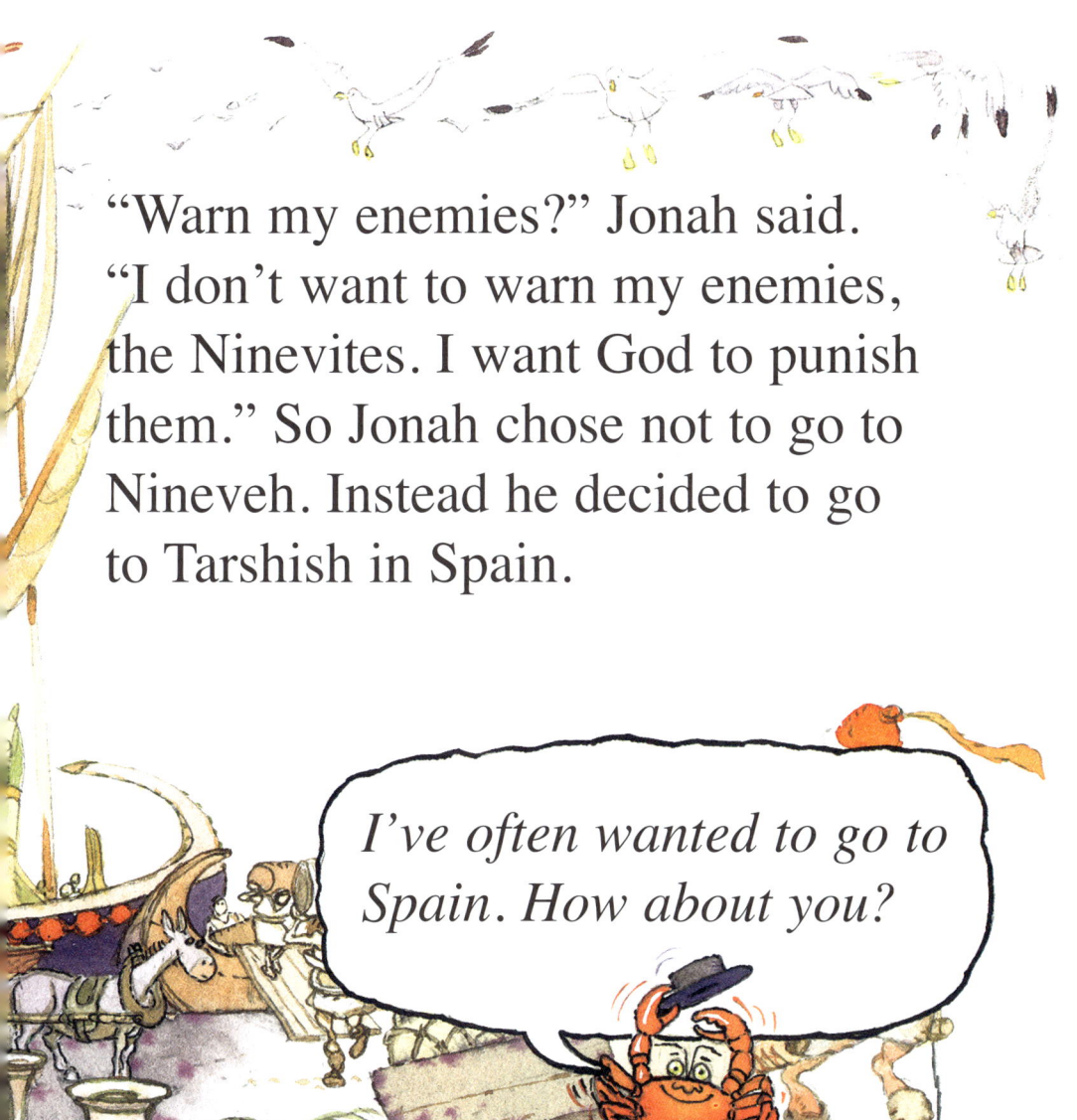

"Warn my enemies?" Jonah said. "I don't want to warn my enemies, the Ninevites. I want God to punish them." So Jonah chose not to go to Nineveh. Instead he decided to go to Tarshish in Spain.

I've often wanted to go to Spain. How about you?

274

Instead of Nineveh, Jonah went to Joppa, got on a ship, and sailed for Spain. He thought this way he could run away from God.

To get somewhere, you can go straight, or you can walk sideways like me. Try it!

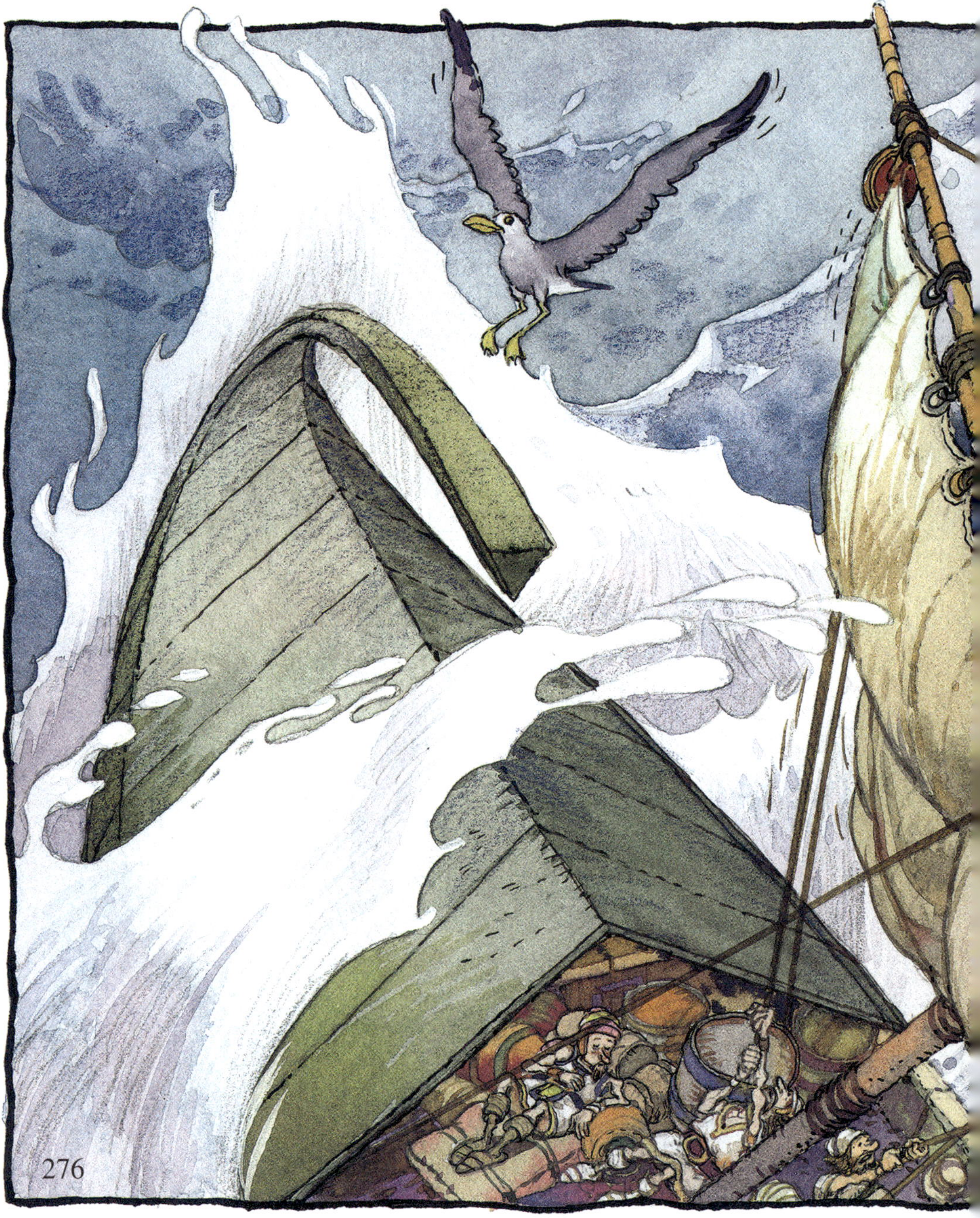

But even Jonah couldn't run away from God. God is everywhere. Jonah disobeyed, so God sent a terrible storm.

Show how the boat went back and forth, up and down. Now show how the boat went WAY UP AND WAY DOWN!!

278

The sailors didn't know what to do! First they threw all the cargo overboard. Then they woke up Jonah. "What did you do to make God send this storm?"

The sailors wanted to know how to stop the storm. The wind was blowing very fast! Try blowing as hard as the wind!

Jonah said, "This storm is all my fault. Throw me overboard and you'll be safe." The sailors didn't want to, but they had no choice.

They picked up Jonah and one, two, three, heave ho! Into the raging sea he went with a great big SPLASH! Can you make bubble sounds (even though you're NOT underwater)?

281

Before he knew it, Jonah was swallowed by a great big whale. GULP!

283

Jonah and the Big Fish

Jonah 1–4

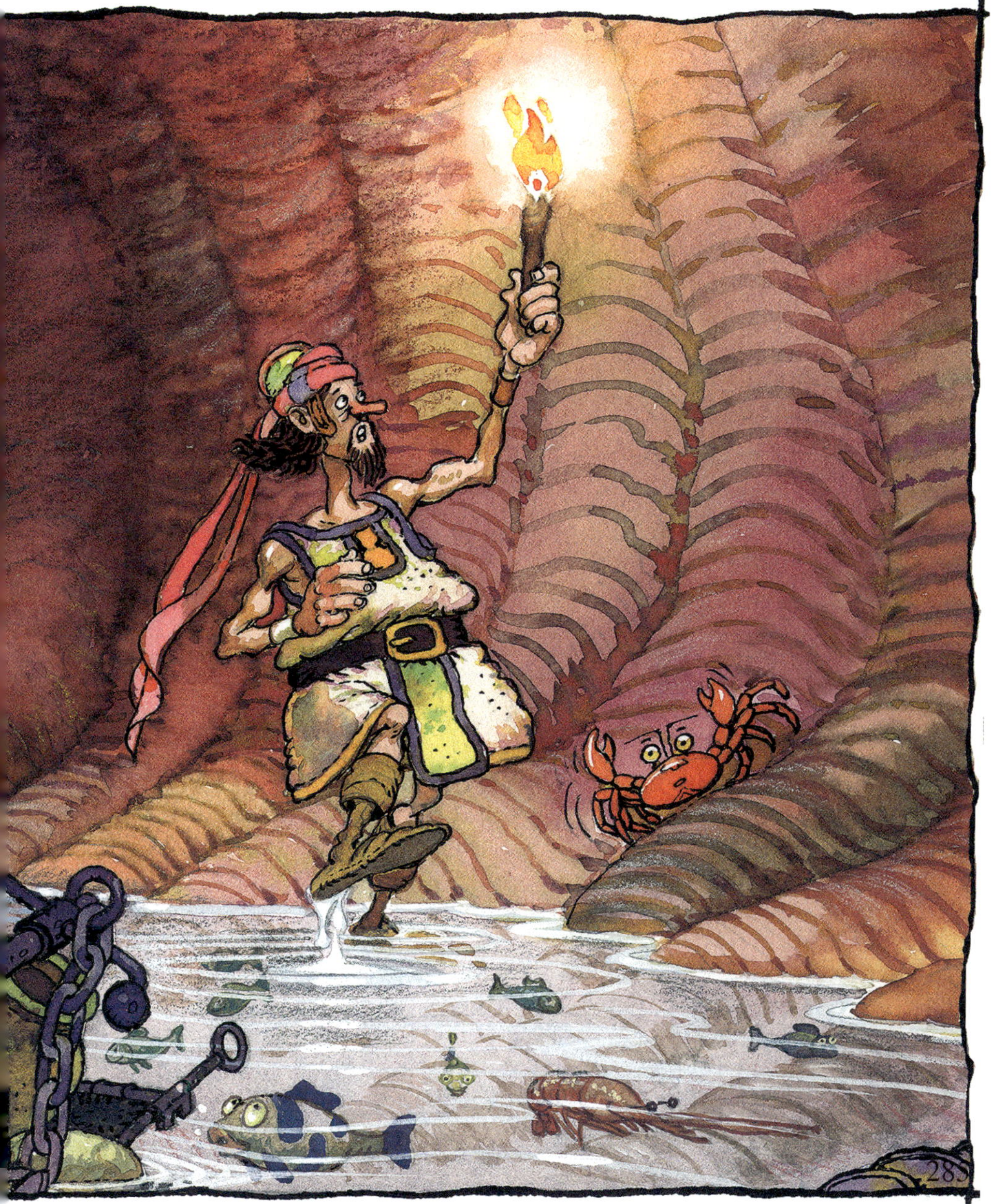

GULP! For three days and nights Jonah stayed in the big fish's belly. Finally Jonah prayed and said he was sorry. Then God had the fish spit him out on a beach.

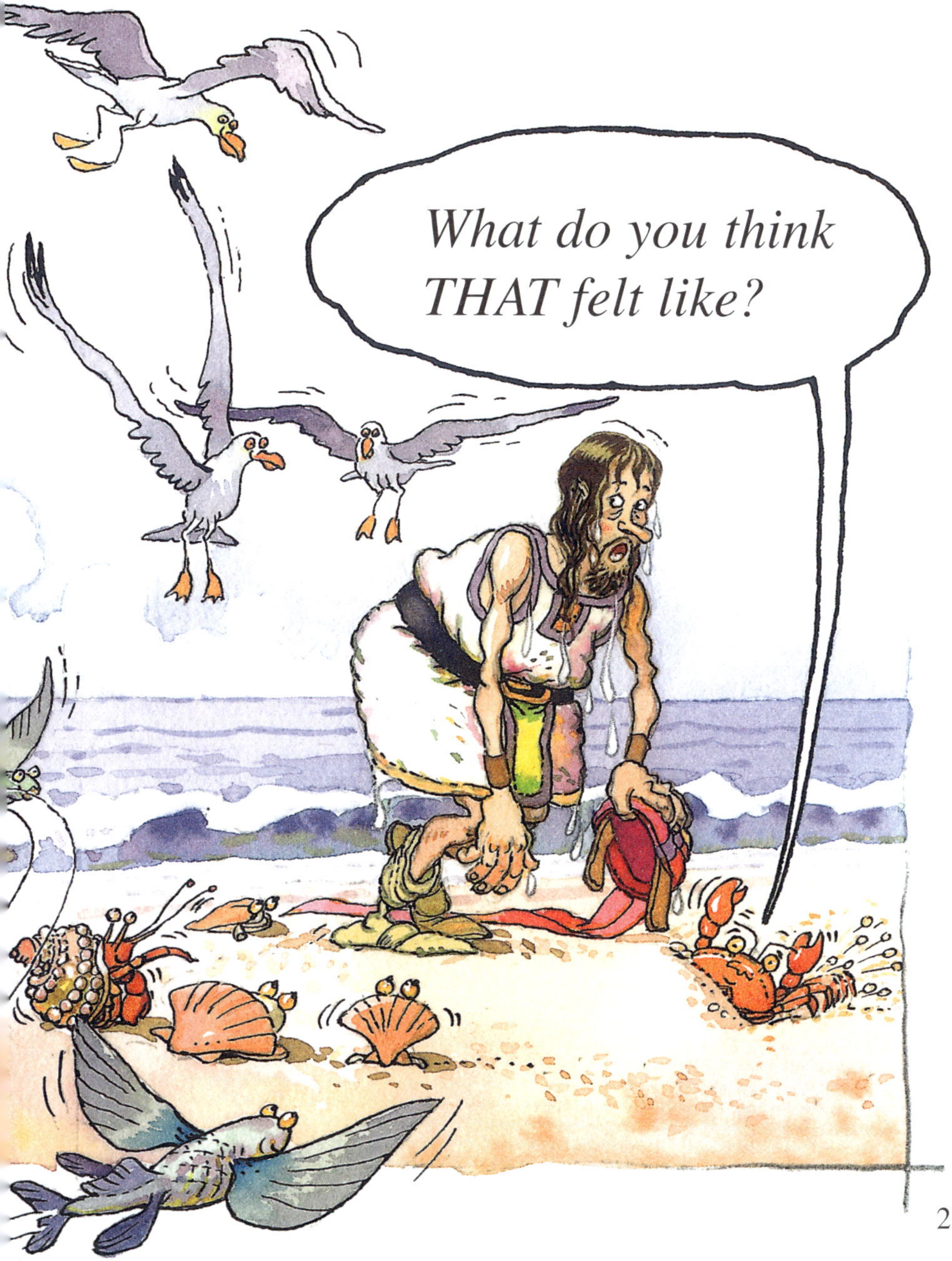
What do you think THAT felt like?

God still wanted Jonah to go to Nineveh. Not Spain, or anywhere else. Nineveh. So this time, what did Jonah do? FINALLY, he went to Nineveh.

Jonah spent one whole day wandering up and down the streets. He told his enemies to live better lives or God would punish them.

289

Guess what? The Ninevites listened!
"Oh! We're so sorry!" they cried.
They put on clothes that looked like
sacks to show God how sorry
they were.

And they meant it, too!

Even the king was sorry. He took off his rich robes and put on sackclothes like the rest of the Ninevites.

God forgave the Ninevites. They heard His message and obeyed.

Everyone prayed and asked God to save them.

And that's what God wanted.

When God chose to forgive the Ninevites, Jonah was not happy. He was mad and went off by himself. God caused a plant to grow and shade Jonah.

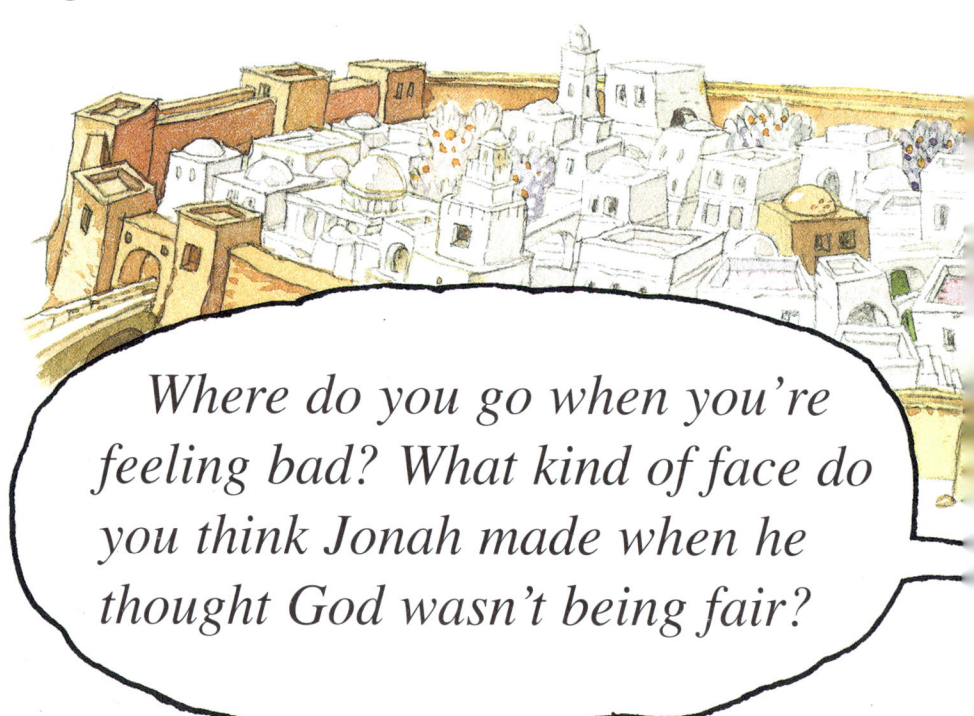

Where do you go when you're feeling bad? What kind of face do you think Jonah made when he thought God wasn't being fair?

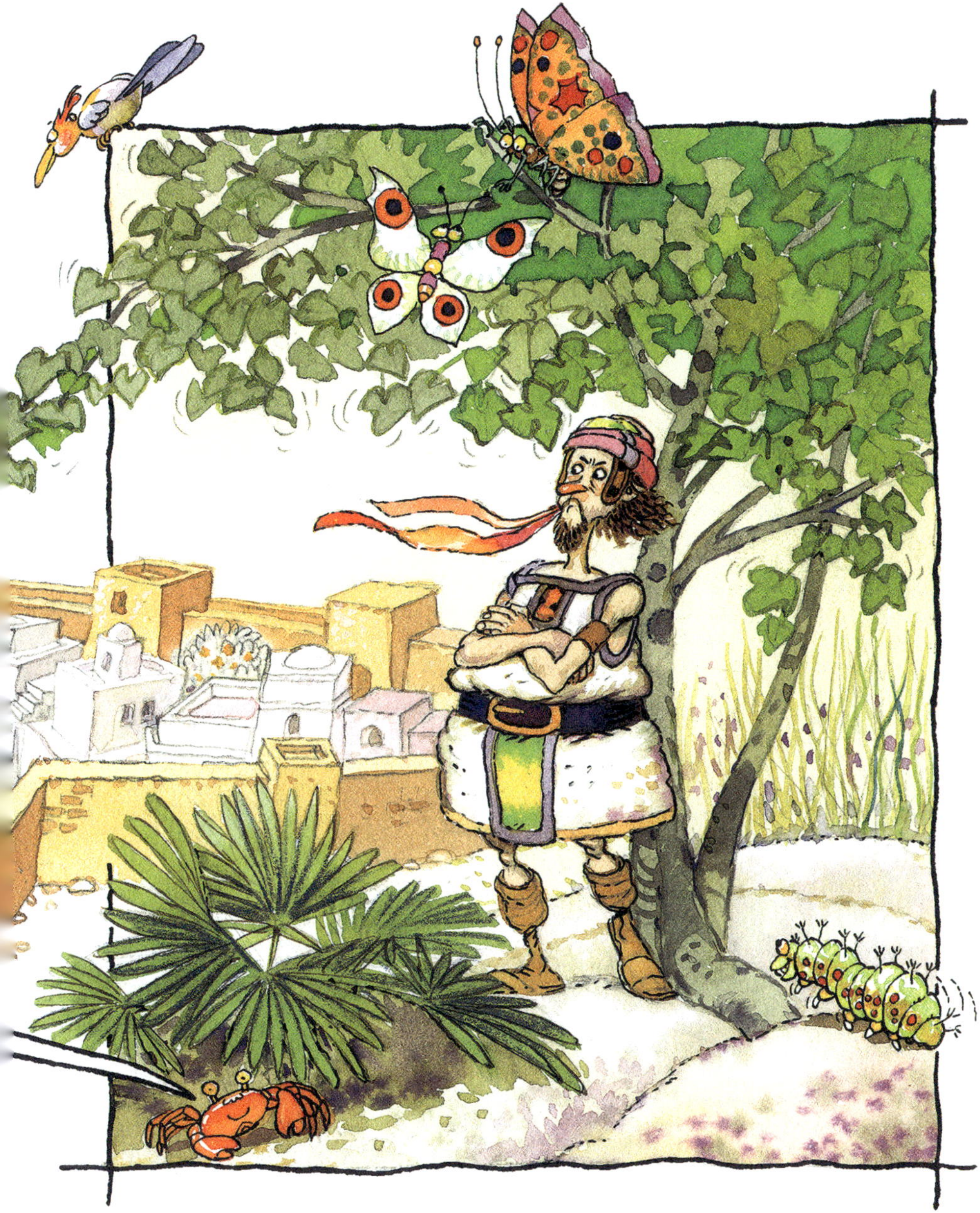

Then God had a worm attack the plant and make it die. Now Jonah was REALLY mad. But God told Jonah, "You care about the plant. Think of how much more *I* care about all those men and women and children. They are why I sent you to Nineveh!"

> *Jonah took a different route to Nineveh. Some of us walk sideways to get somewhere. Like walking sideways, Jonah's way was different, but he got there in the end. And he learned a WHALE of a lesson.*

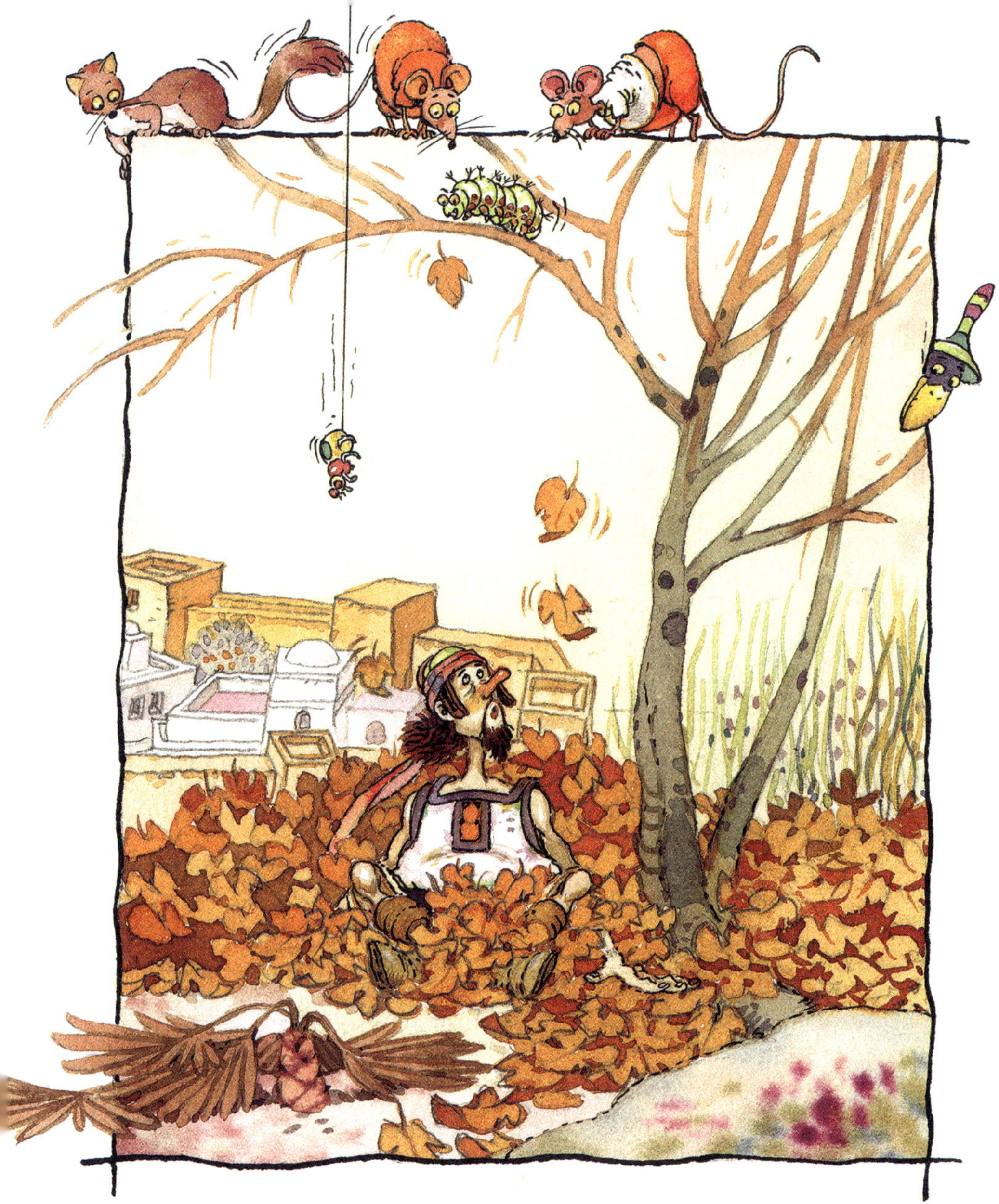

Daniel the Prisoner

2 Kings 25; 2 Chronicles 36; Jeremiah 39–40, 52; Daniel 1

A long time ago, there was a young boy named Daniel who was very brave.

During a terrible war, an enemy army attacked Jerusalem and took many of God's people prisoner. Poor Daniel! The soldiers marched him off to Babylon, far, far away.

Some say Daniel was a prince of Jerusalem. Prince or prisoner, Daniel swore never to forget his home or his family. What did Daniel do? He talked to God.

The king of Babylon was called Nebuchadnezzar. He ordered the soldiers to search through the many prisoners. "Look for the strongest and cleverest boys. Then send them to my special school!"

Can you say "Nebuchadnezzar"? Not with your mouth full! Where is the king?

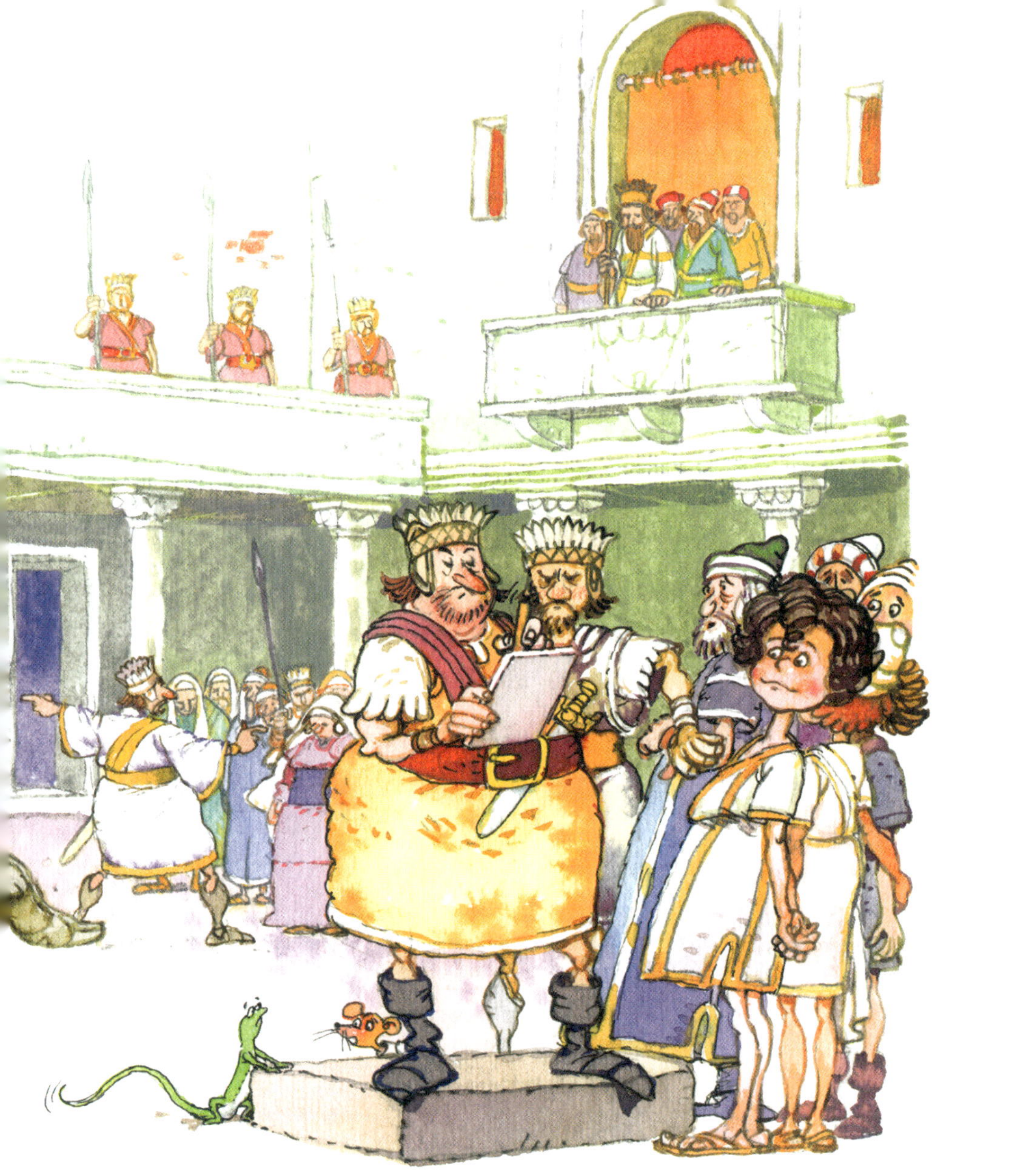

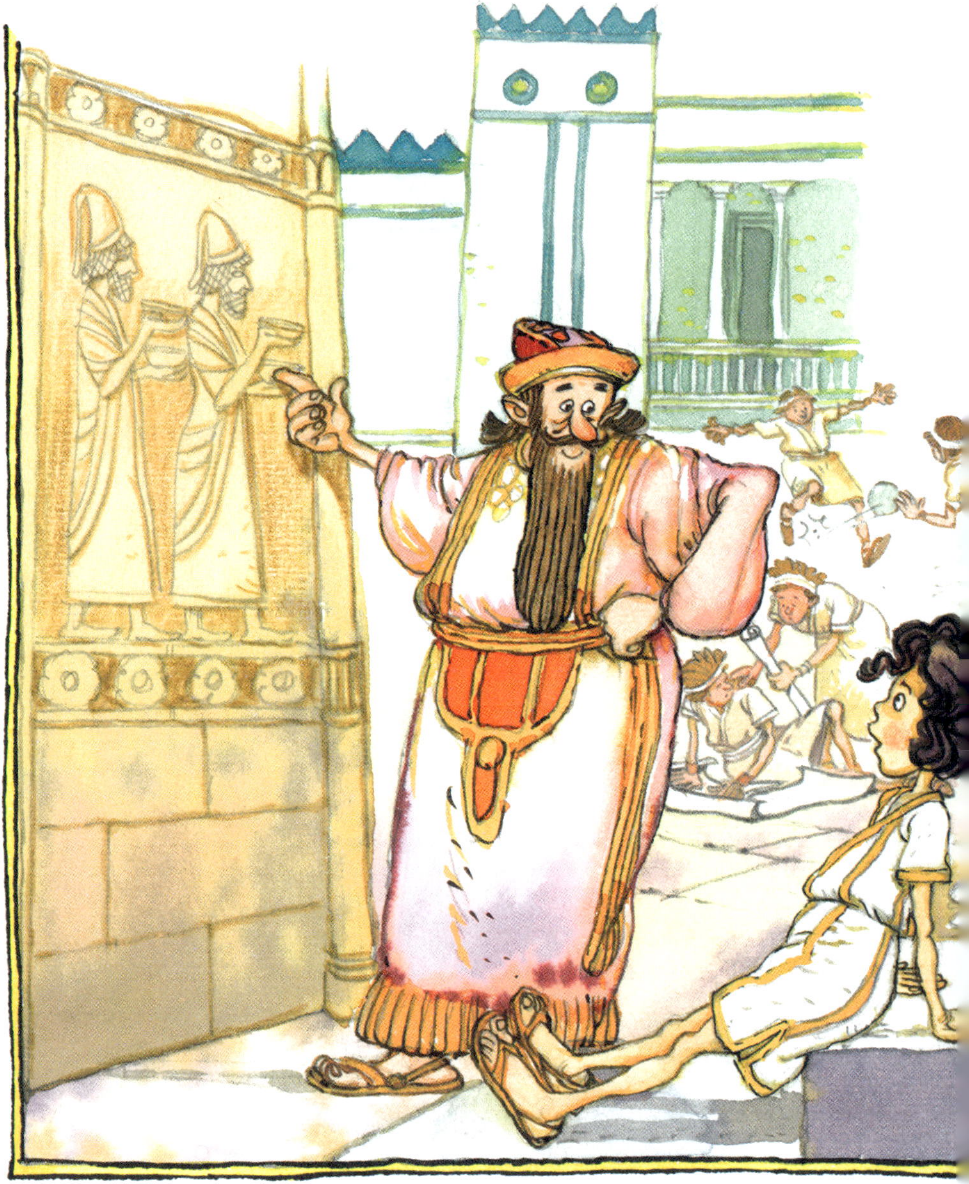

At the king's special school, Daniel and his friends had to read Babylonian and write Babylonian.

They even had new Babylonian names. Daniel was called "Belteshazzar." How do you say THAT?

What makes YOU different?

They were told to eat like Babylonians, drink like Babylonians, and pray like Babylonians. But Daniel told his teachers, "No! We're not like you. We're different."

Daniel told his friends, "Remember who we are! We are different from the Babylonians. We must remember what our parents taught us!"

Daniel and his friends were trying to follow God's rules for His people. Name one thing your parents have taught YOU.

Daniel and the Lions

Daniel 5–6

Years later, Nebuchadnezzar died. When his son, the new king, threw a party, a strange hand appeared!

יהודים

This strange hand wrote something on the wall. No one knew what it said. The king sent for Daniel, who asked God what it meant.

Daniel said it was a message from God. God was not pleased with the new king, who worshiped gold and silver more than God. The writing said that God had judged the kingdom and the king.

The king rewarded Daniel, but this did not change the will of God.

The king died that very night!

The next king, Darius, loved Daniel. But Daniel's enemies tricked the king and had Daniel arrested.

Poor Daniel was an old man by this time. And here he was, a prisoner again.

"You must punish him for praying to his God," these enemies told the king.

The guards threw Daniel into a pit with lions! But God sent an angel to shut the lions' mouths. He stayed there all night.

RROOAAAARRRR!
Hey, I can't open my mouth!
MMMMHHHMMM!

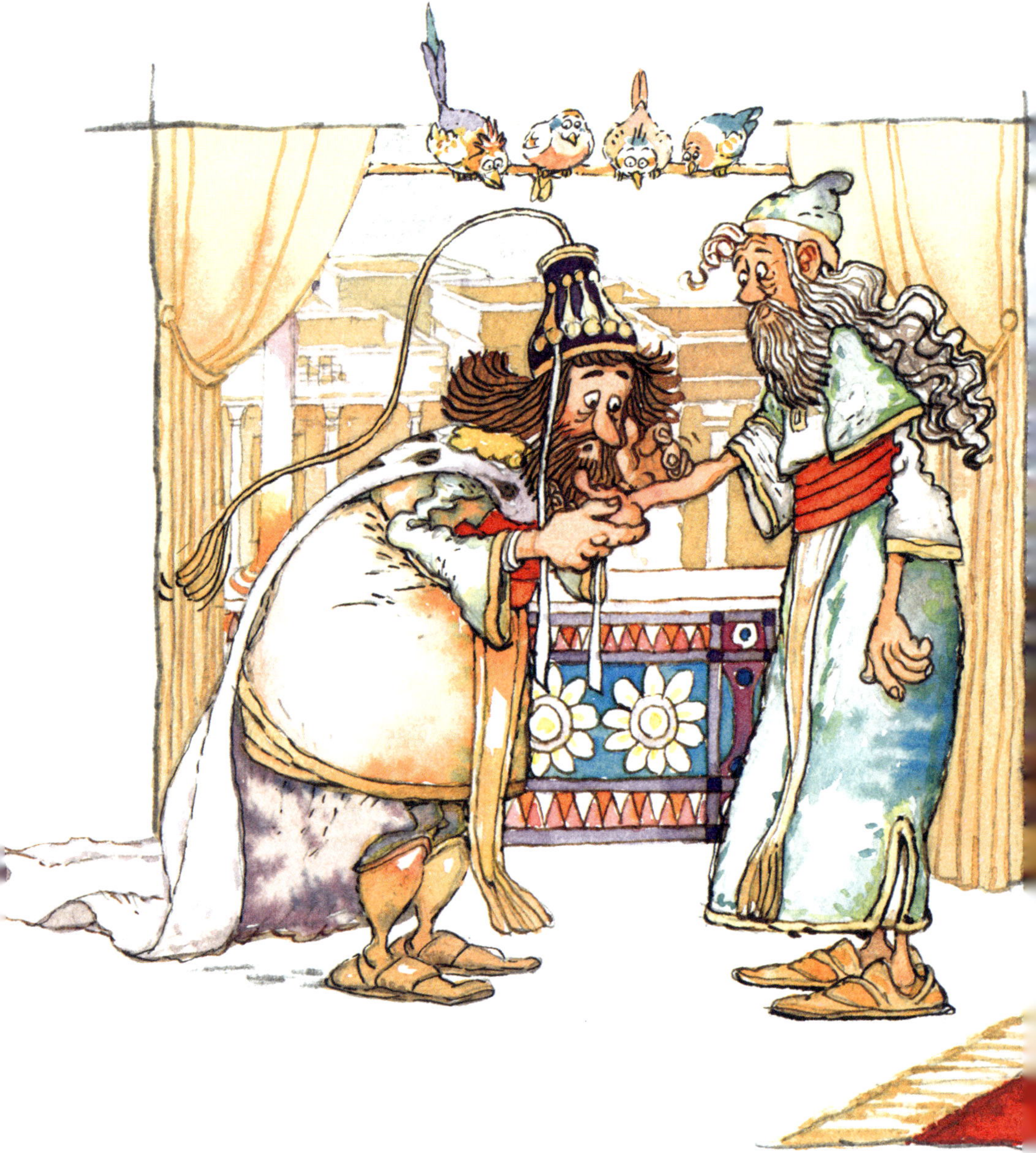

In the morning Daniel did not even have one scratch on him. "God has kept me safe," he told the king.

Why was Daniel different? What did he do every day, no matter if it landed him with the lions? Daniel talked to God! Did YOU talk to God today?

Esther the Beautiful

Esther 1

There once was a king who searched far and wide for a queen.

The king had the most beautiful women brought to the palace. There they waited a year to hear who would be chosen. They ate the best food, wore the prettiest makeup and sweetest perfumes, and were given the best massages.

Rub the shoulders of the person reading to you. Now it's your turn!

323

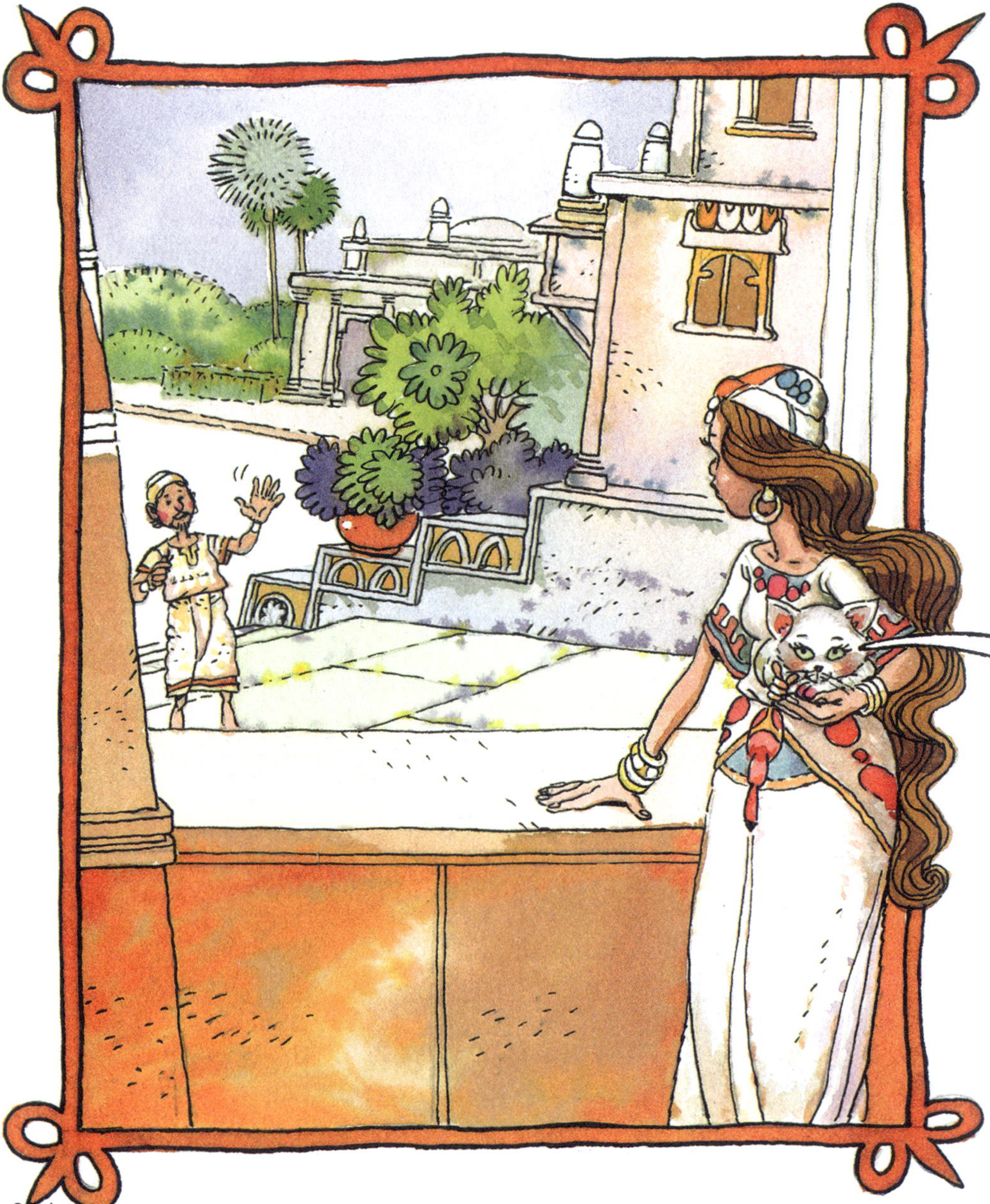

One of the girls was named Esther. She was very special, and not just because she was so beautiful. Esther was special because she was keeping a special secret. Esther's secret was that she was a Jew, one of God's chosen people.

What was your most fun, all-time favorite secret? Come on, you can tell me!

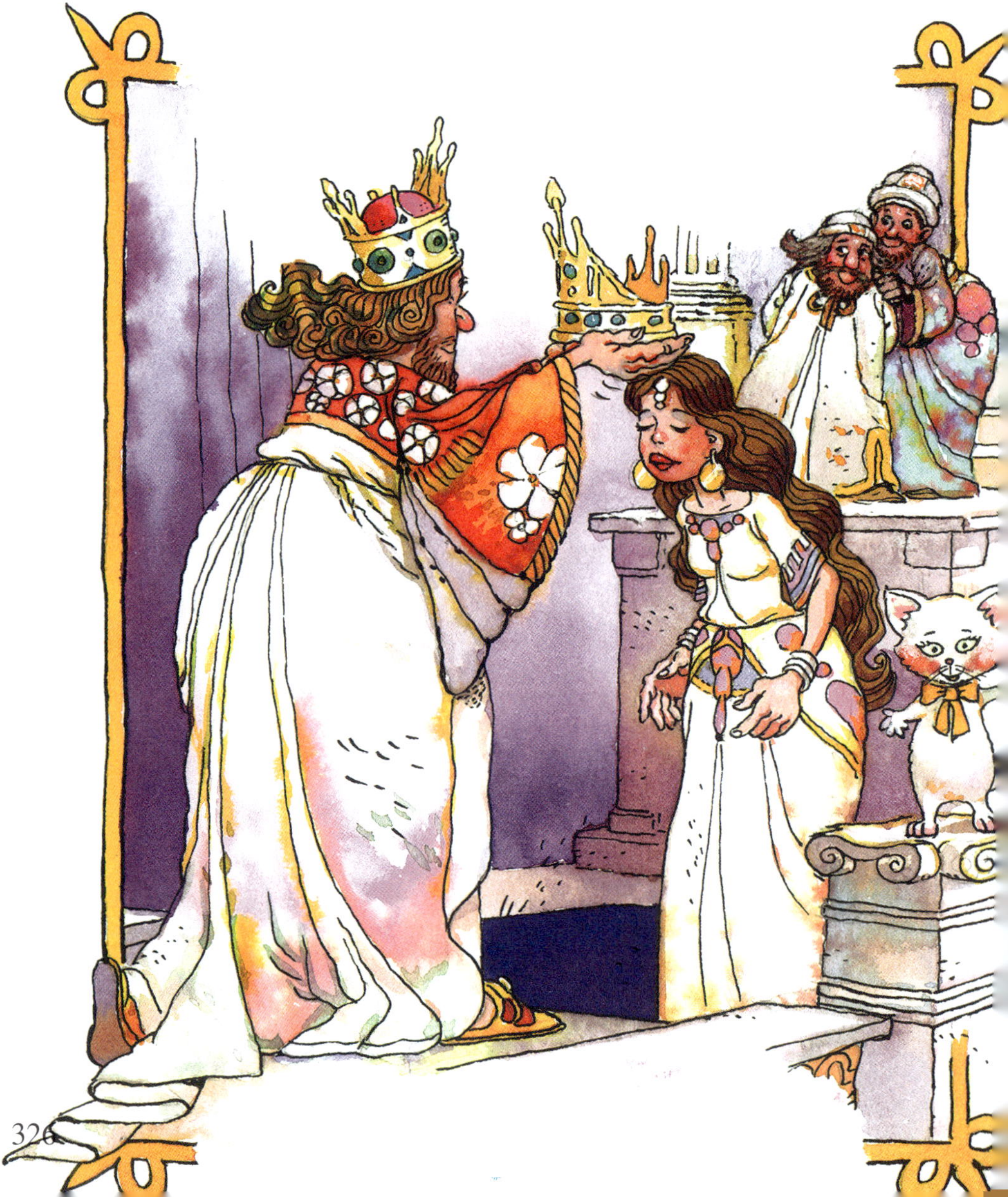

When it was Esther's turn to meet the king, there was no contest! He chose her and she became Queen Esther.

What do you think was so beautiful about Esther? What do you think God saw in Esther that was beautiful?

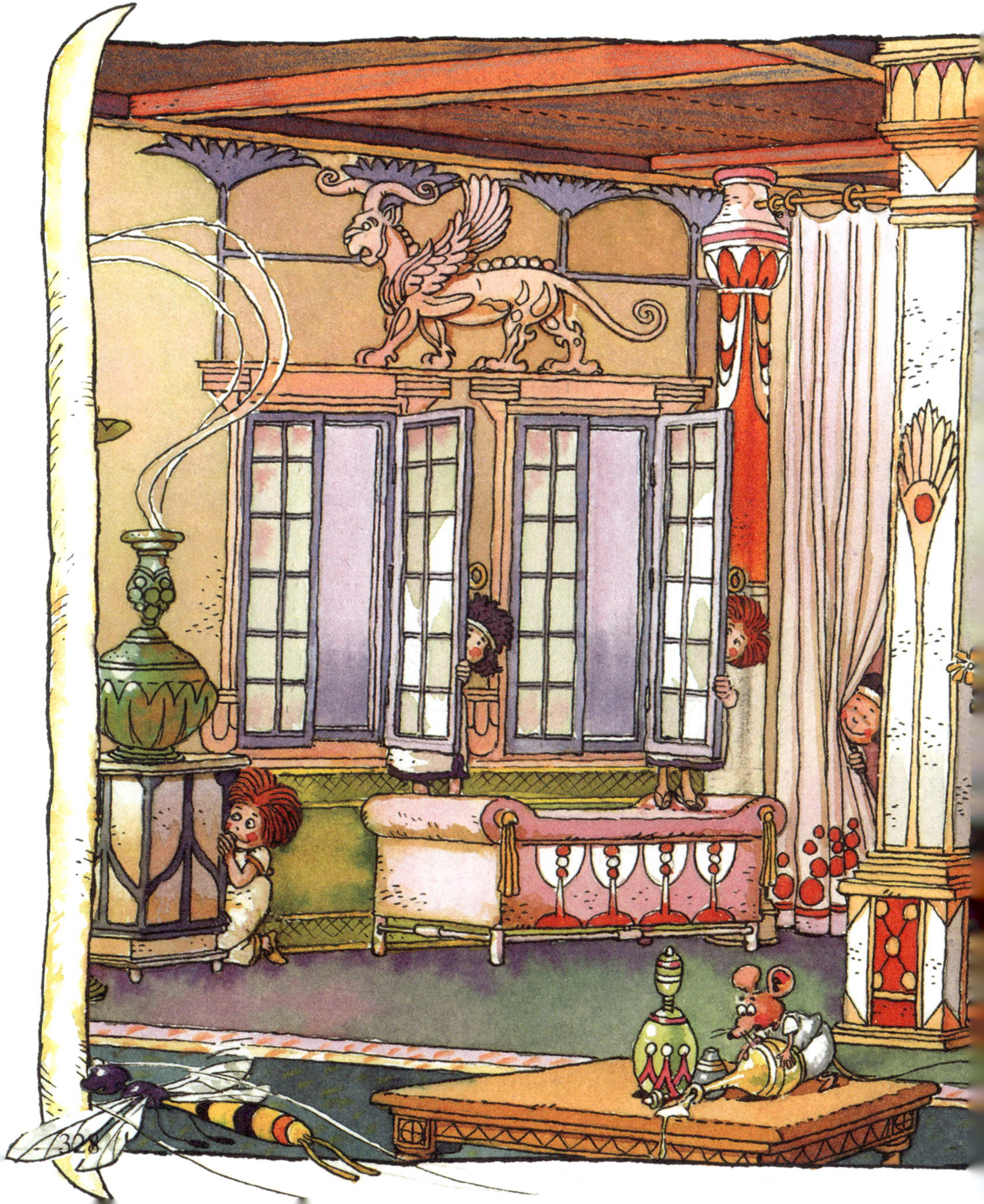

Queen Esther Saves Her People
Esther 2–7

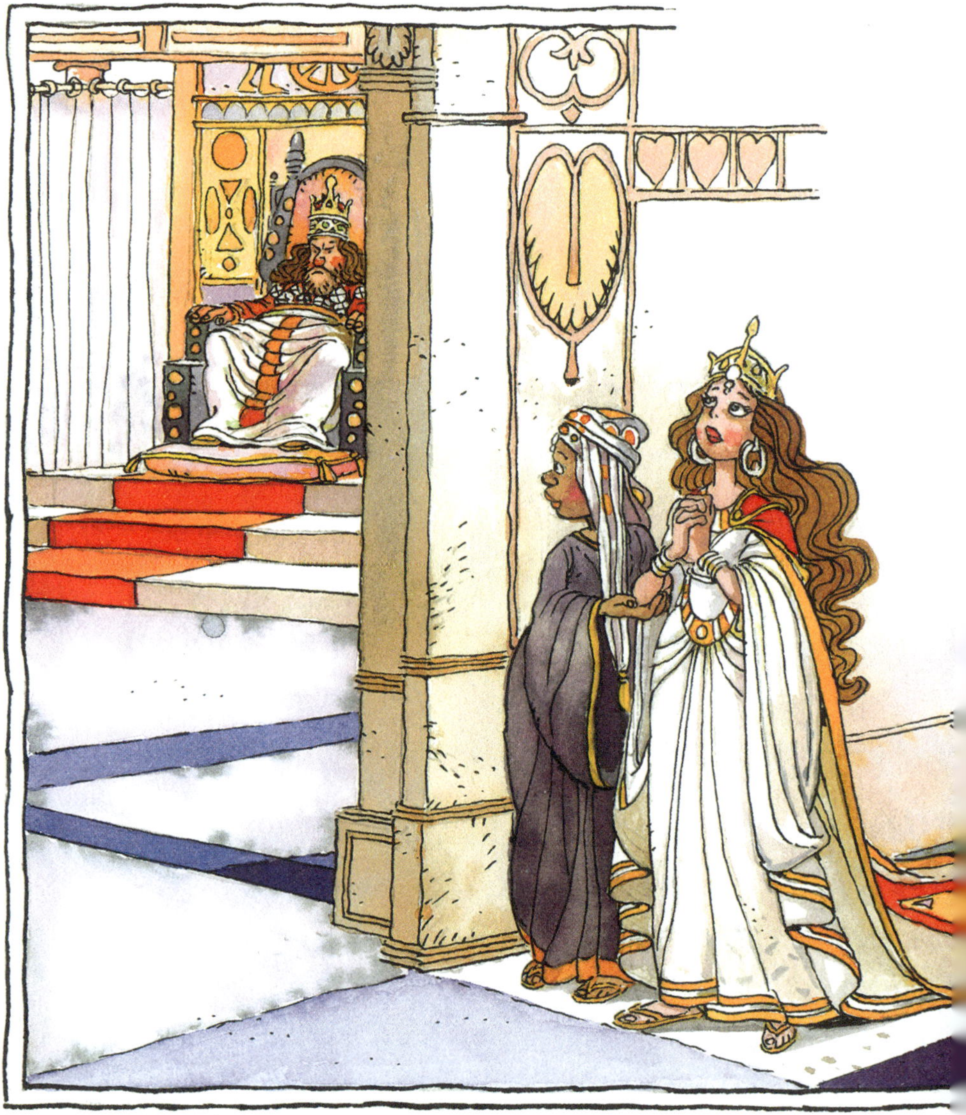

The king loved Esther, but did not know she was Jewish. When a new and terrible law ordered all Jews to be killed, Esther prayed to God, then went to the king.

Esther knew the king could have her killed for coming to see him without being invited. Would he be angry?

The king smiled when he saw Esther. "Of course I will see you, Esther. What do you wish from me?" Esther trusted God. She asked the king to dinner, and there, she told the king everything!

If you were the king or queen, what would you order for dinner every day?

333

The king helped Esther. Afterward, he celebrated by giving gifts to the poor. Then he threw a huge party and called it the Feast of Purim, when God used Esther the brave and beautiful to save the Jewish people.

> *The Feast of Purim is still celebrated to this day, all thanks to courageous Esther, who trusted God to save her people.*

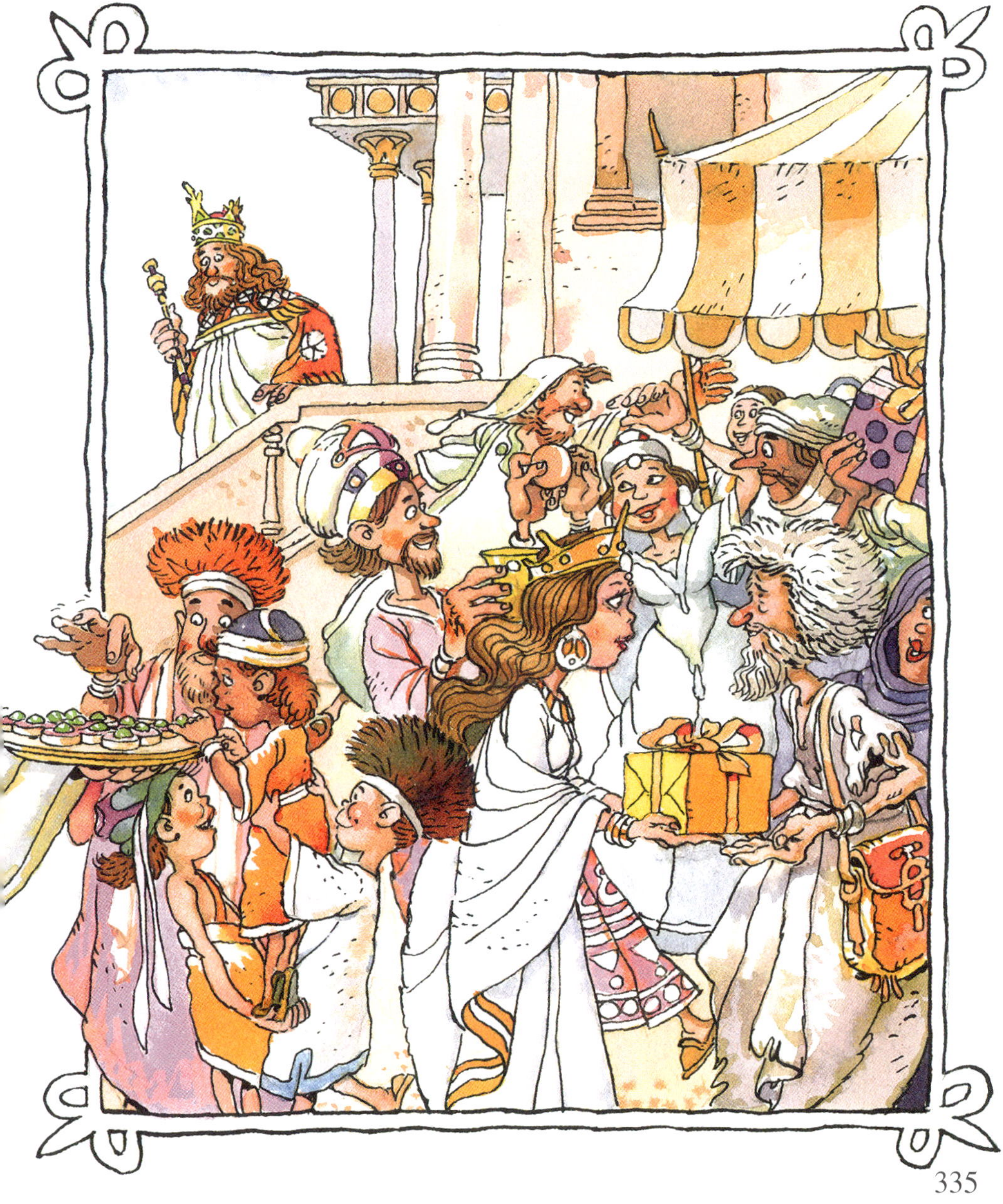

THE NEW TESTAMENT

Mary and Joseph

Luke 1; Matthew 1

The Christmas story begins with a girl named Mary waking up to a bright light. An angel told her, "Mary, you are very special. God has chosen you to become the mother of Jesus, God's Son."

Close your eyes. Hold your breath. Imagine an angel standing by your bed. What would he say?

Mary was going to marry Joseph. When she told him about her baby, he shook his head. "I don't understand."

What would you do if you did not understand something? Whom could you go to for help?

God sent an angel to Joseph in a dream. The angel said, "Don't be afraid to make Mary your wife. She is telling the truth about the baby. You will call him Jesus."

And that's who Christmas is about: Baby Jesus.

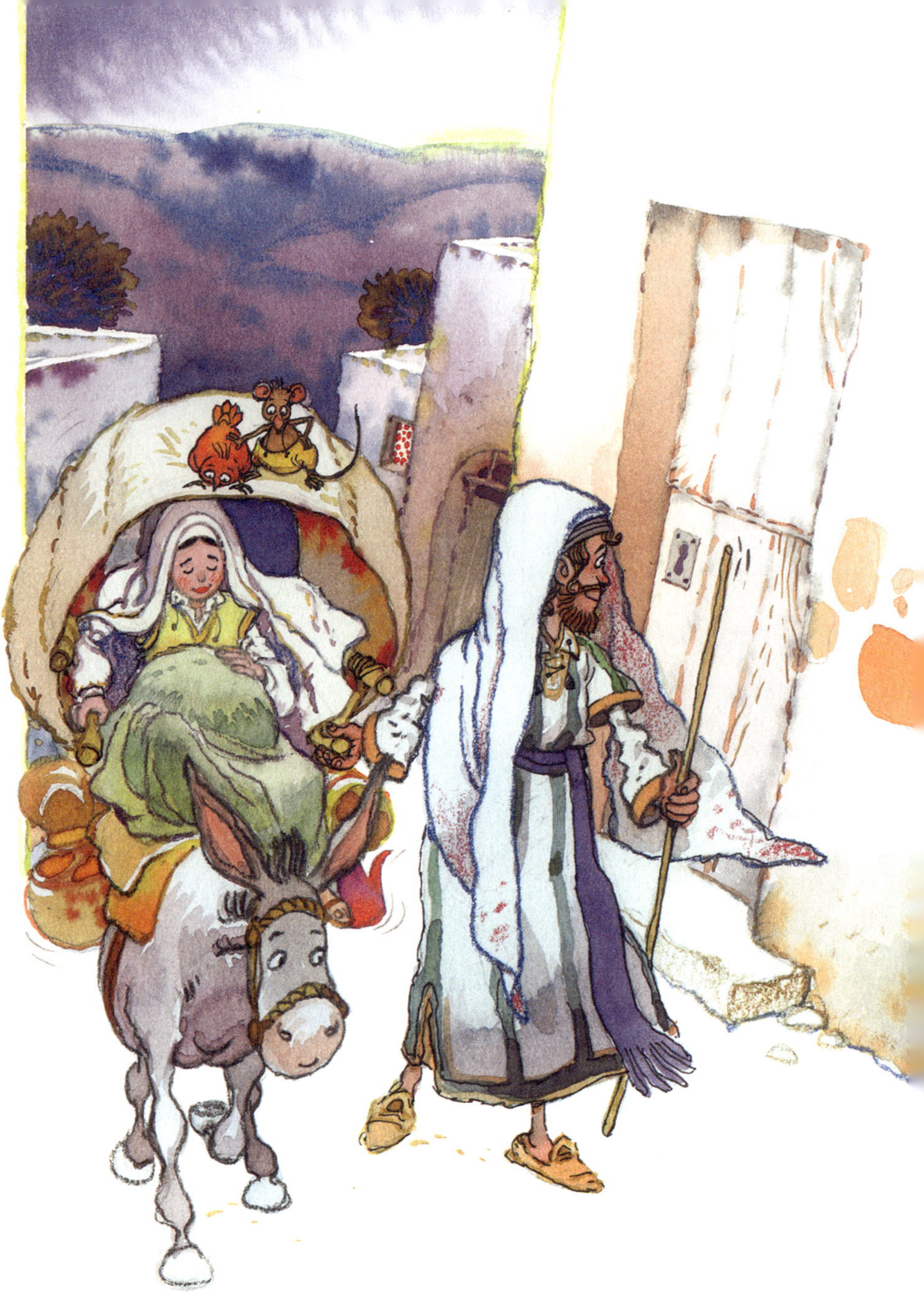

When Jesus was almost ready to be born, Mary and Joseph had to make a long trip. Mary rode a donkey all the way from Nazareth to Bethlehem.

Jesus was growing in Mary's tummy. Do you know anyone who is going to have a baby? You can pray for that baby now.

When Mary and Joseph arrived in Bethlehem, there was no place for them to stay! The city was full of people. Everywhere they tried, they heard the same thing.

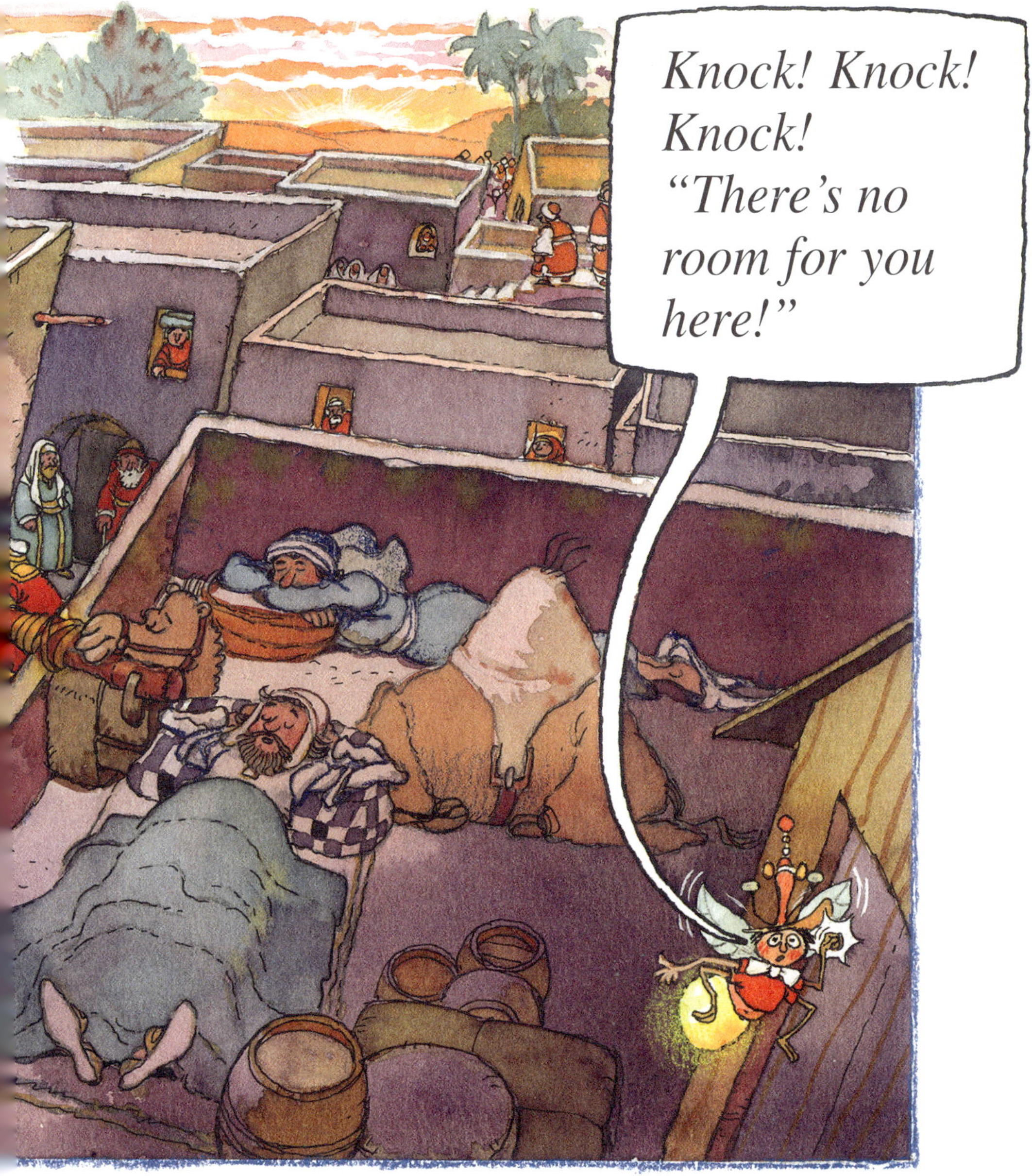
Knock! Knock! Knock!
"There's no room for you here!"

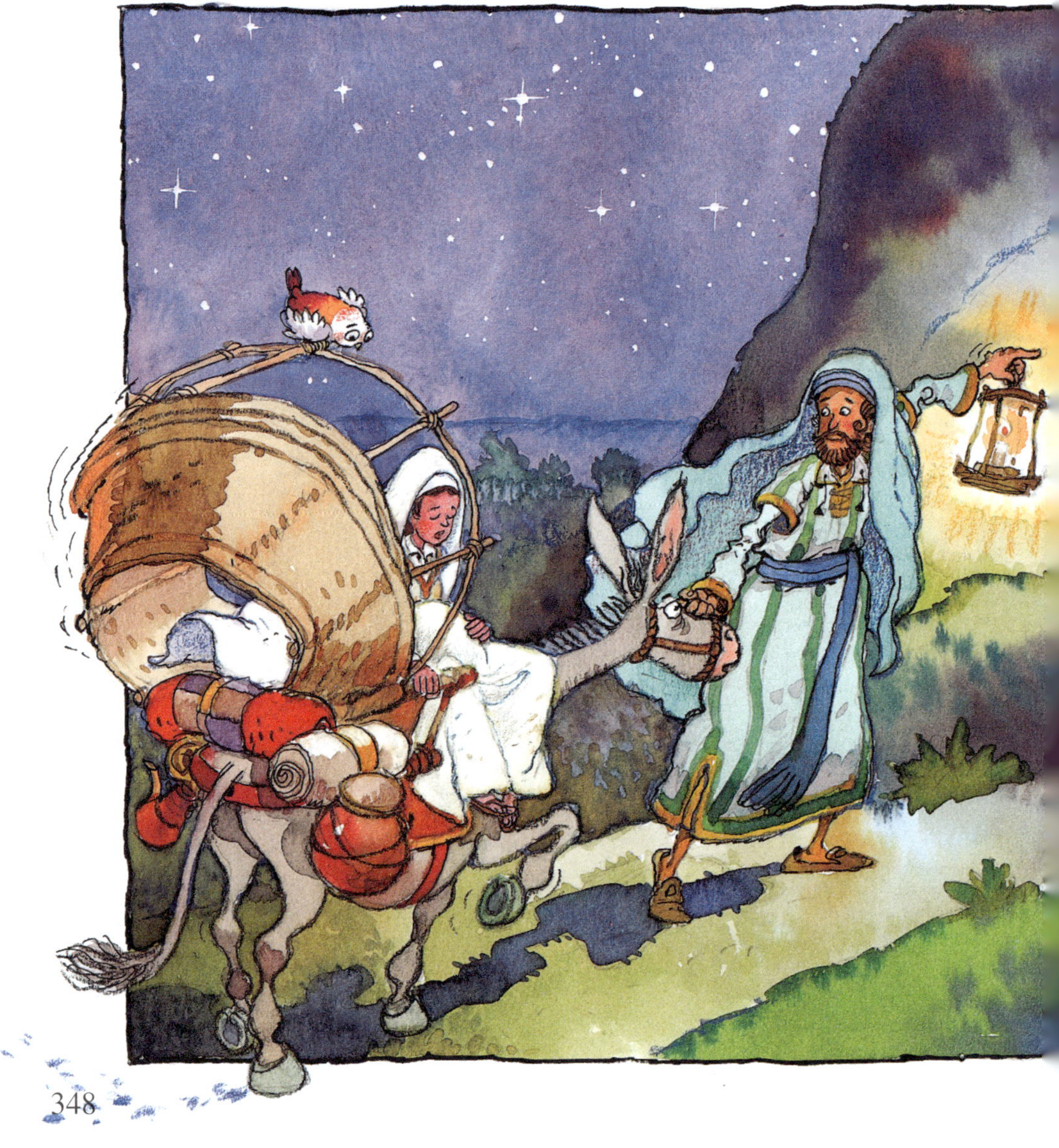

Where would Jesus be born? What did the cow say? And the goat?

The First Christmas

Matthew 1–2; Luke 2

On the night Jesus was born, shepherds in the nearby hills saw angels singing in the sky. "Glory to God! A Savior is born!"

The shepherds said, "Look!"

That night the shepherds ran to a cave in the hillside. "Look!"

Inside, they found a stable, two people, and the tiny, newborn Baby Jesus.

Mary and Joseph took Baby Jesus to the temple. An old man named Simeon blessed Jesus. He said, "Now I have seen the Light who will save all people." An old woman named Anna said, "Yes. He is the Savior."

What are the two other names Jesus is called here?

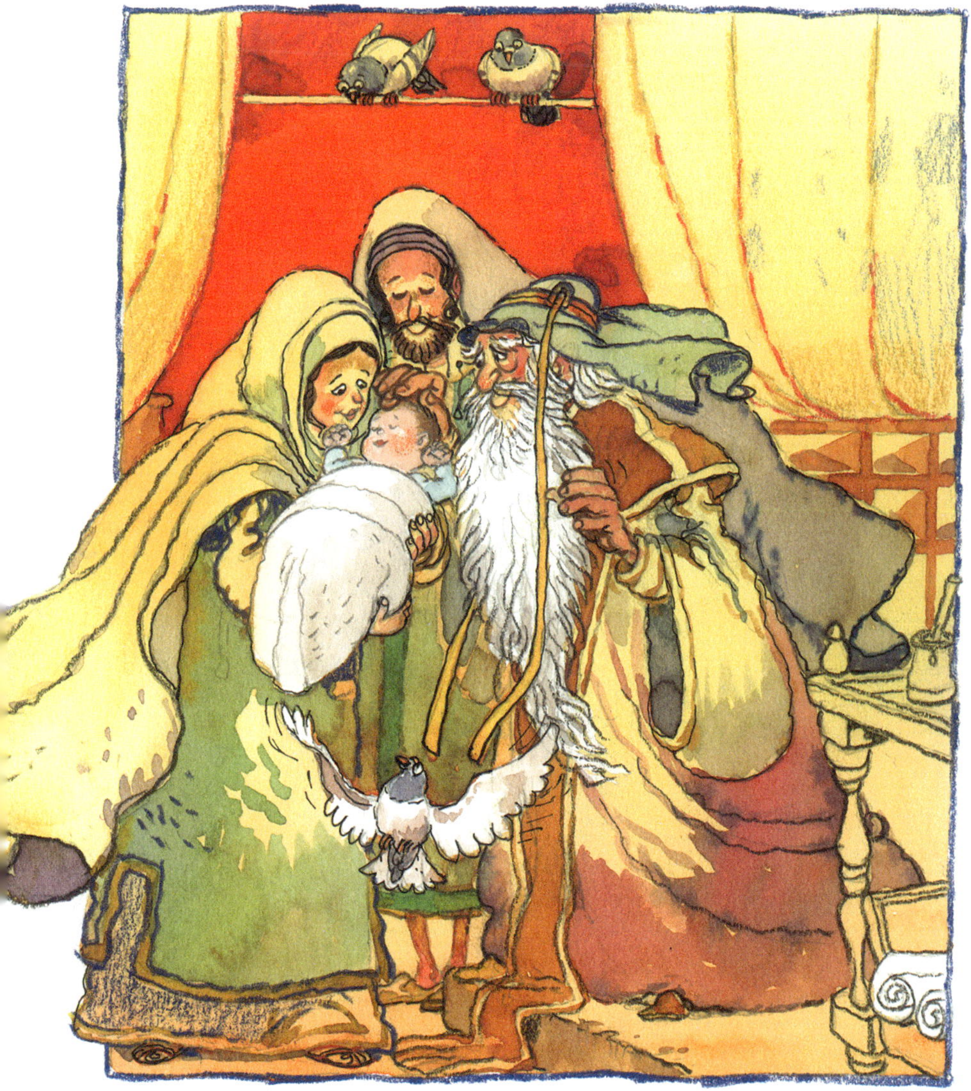

Three wise men who lived far away from Bethlehem saw a giant star. They rode their camels a long way to find out what the bright star meant. They called Baby Jesus the King of the Jews.

Lie down under a Christmas tree and squint your eyes, then maybe the lights will look like stars.

Were the presents more important than the baby?

These three wise men brought Jesus fantastic gifts fit for a king. They gave Jesus gold.

And they gave Jesus a rich perfume called myrrh, and incense, which smells sweet when burned.

Jesus is the Light who helps us see, the Light who shows us the way. THAT'S who Christmas is about: Baby Jesus.

Jesus is called Light of the World. On this first Christmas, Jesus was God's Christmas present to us.

361

The Miracles of Jesus

Matthew 9; Mark 2; Luke 5, 17; John 2, 11

Mary once asked Jesus to help at a wedding when the wine was all gone. So Jesus turned water into wine! A miracle is something God makes happen, even if people think it won't.

363

Once, when Jesus was inside a house teaching, somebody cut a hole in the ceiling! Four men lowered a man down who could not walk. Jesus made him better.

Reach up high and try to touch your ceiling. Do you need some help?

There once were ten very sick men.
"Please help us!" they begged Jesus.
So Jesus did. He made them better.

One day, a sick woman reached through the crowd and touched Jesus' robe. He felt her touch and said, "Your faith has made you whole." And she was healed!

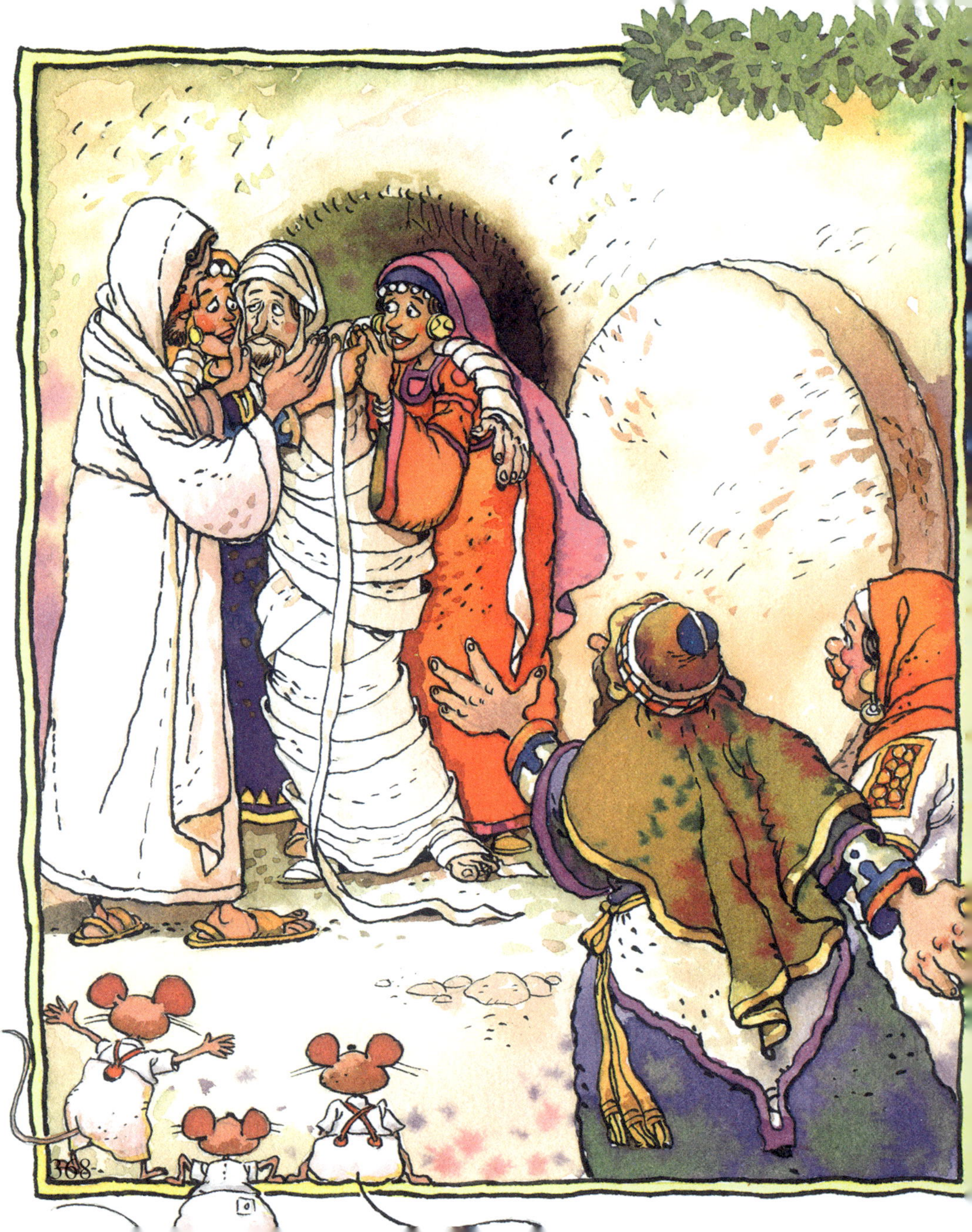

Mary, Martha, and their brother Lazarus were all good friends of Jesus. Once, when Jesus was away, Lazarus became very sick and died. But Jesus came back and made Lazarus live again!

What is a miracle? YOU are a miracle! Jesus made you and that is the most special miracle of all!

Simon Peter the Rock

Matthew 4, 5–10, 12, 14–16, 19–20;
Mark 1, 3, 6, 8, 10;
Luke 4–9, 11, 18;
John 1, 3–4, 6, 9;
Acts 8–12, 15;
Galatians 2;
1 and 2 Peter

What does a fisherman catch?

There once was a fisherman named Simon. One day, Simon was fishing with his brother. Jesus sailed out to them in another boat and said, "Come, follow Me." Jesus chose Simon plus eleven other men to be His closest followers, or disciples.

Can you count how many disciples there were?

Simon and the other apostles followed Jesus from village to village, listening and learning.

Jesus taught: Love is the greatest commandment.

The crowds grew larger every time Jesus taught. "Follow Me," He called to the people.

Play follow-the-leader. March around the room, then turn around. Now who's following?

Simon watched Jesus help the blind people to see and the disabled to walk. Simon could not believe his eyes.

Try taking five careful steps with your eyes closed. Now open them wide. What do you see?

Simon followed Jesus for over two years. The more he listened to Jesus and knew His heart, the more he loved Him. One day, Jesus told him, "Your name is Simon, but from now on you will be called Peter."

Jesus said, "Someday you will lead the people who follow Me. They are My church. You will become the rock, or foundation, on which the church is built." Peter means *Rock*.

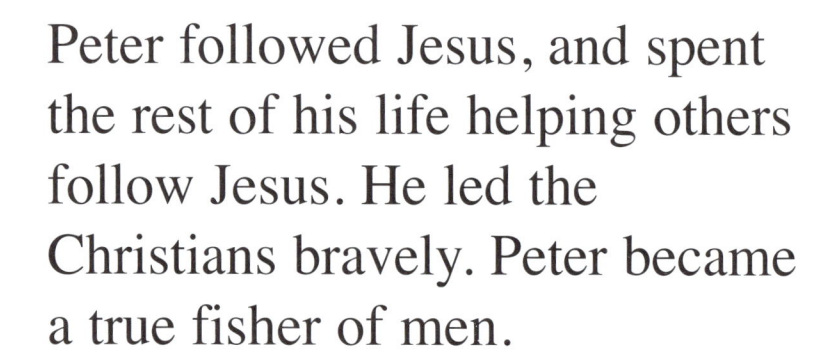

Peter followed Jesus, and spent the rest of his life helping others follow Jesus. He led the Christians bravely. Peter became a true fisher of men.

What does a fisher of men catch?

The Stories of Jesus

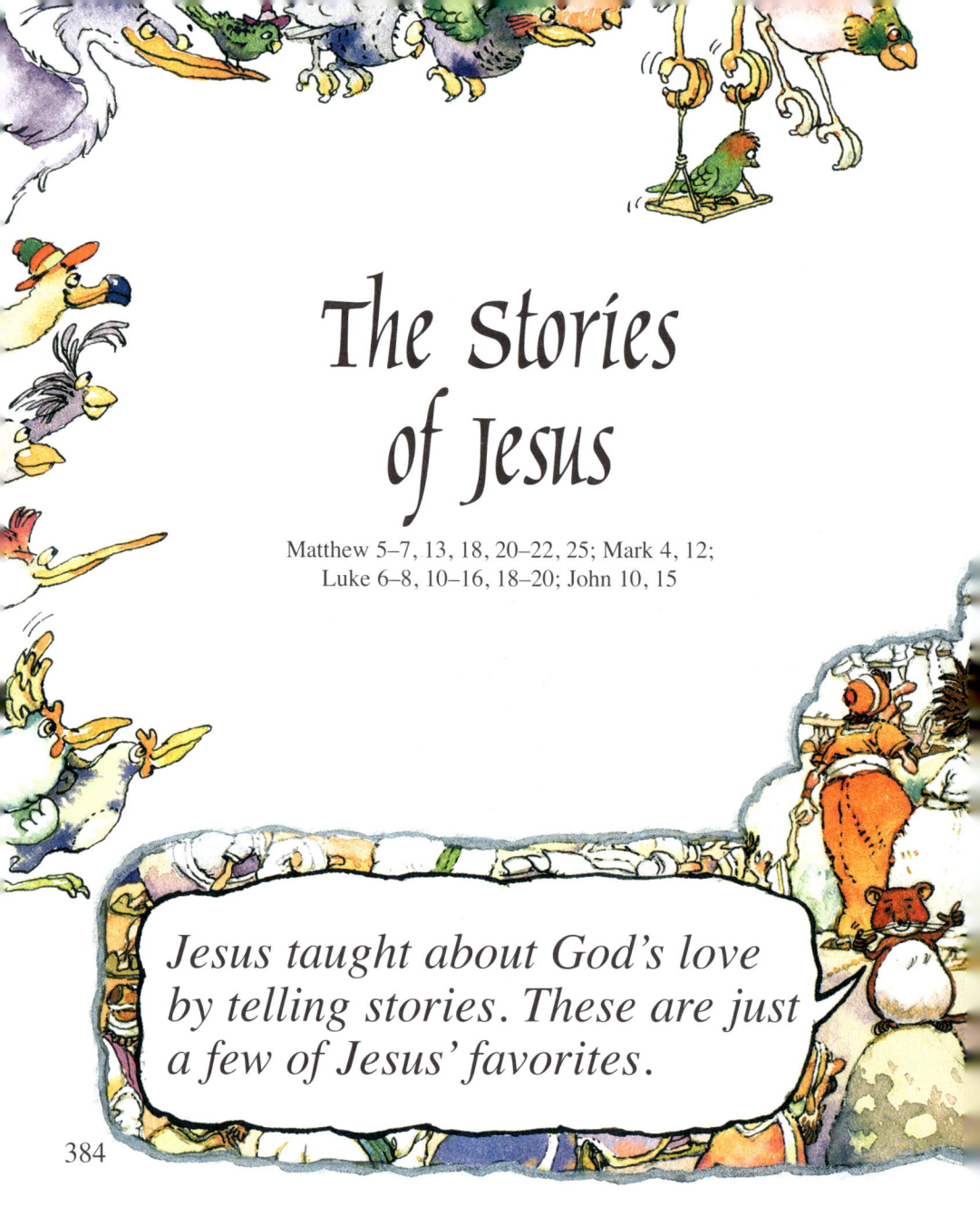

Matthew 5–7, 13, 18, 20–22, 25; Mark 4, 12;
Luke 6–8, 10–16, 18–20; John 10, 15

Jesus taught about God's love by telling stories. These are just a few of Jesus' favorites.

385

Jesus said not to worry about food and clothes. God knows what people need. Jesus told His followers they were more valuable than the flowers that grow and birds that fly. Yet God takes good care of the flowers and birds, too.

What color of flowers and birds did you see today?

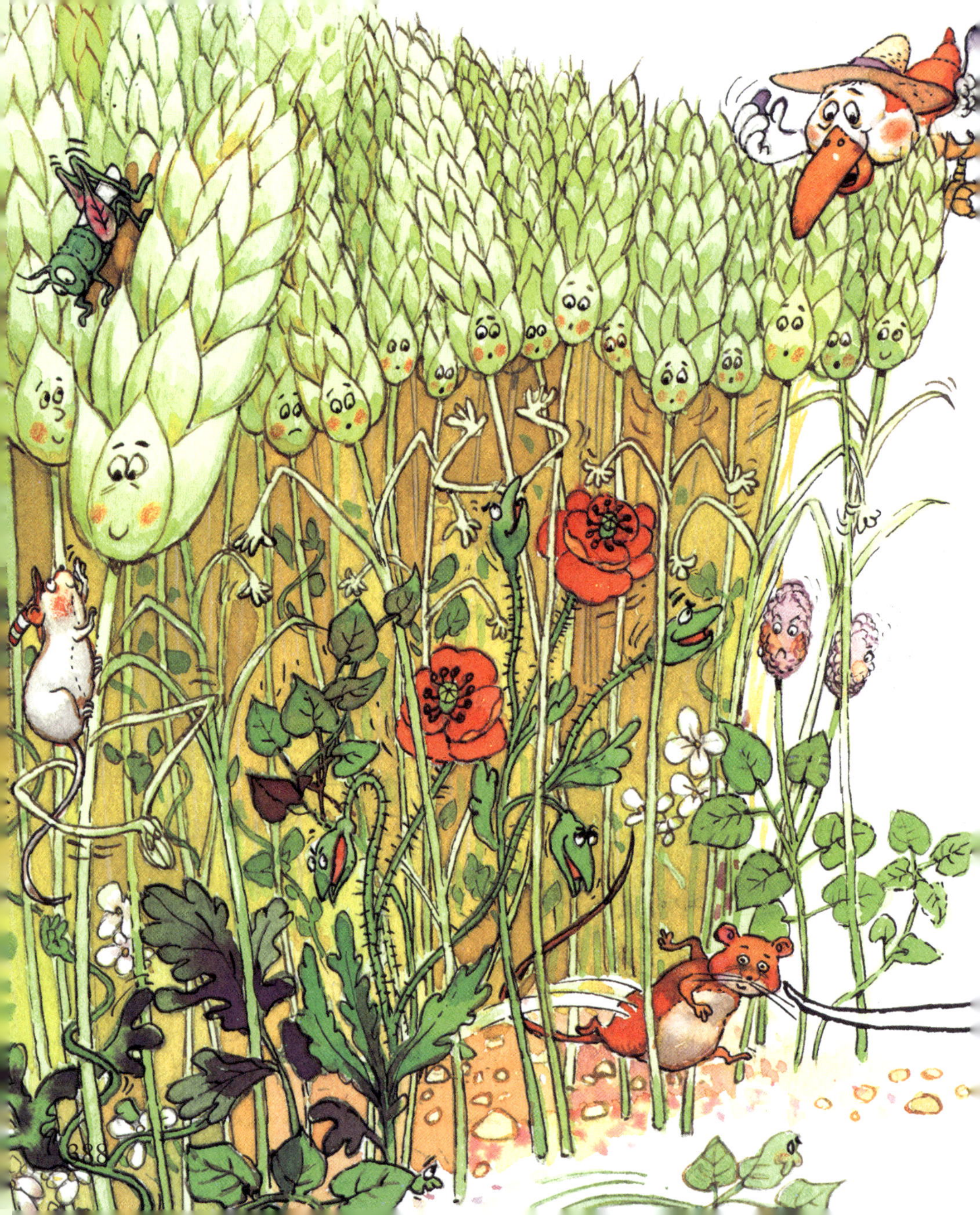

In another story, Jesus said the kingdom of heaven was like a wheat field. The farmer's enemy had planted weeds alongside the wheat. Jesus said both the bad and good plants could grow together. Those who believe in Him, or the good plants, would be separated and grow even stronger.

Jesus was comparing the wheat field to the world. Have you ever planted something and watched it grow?

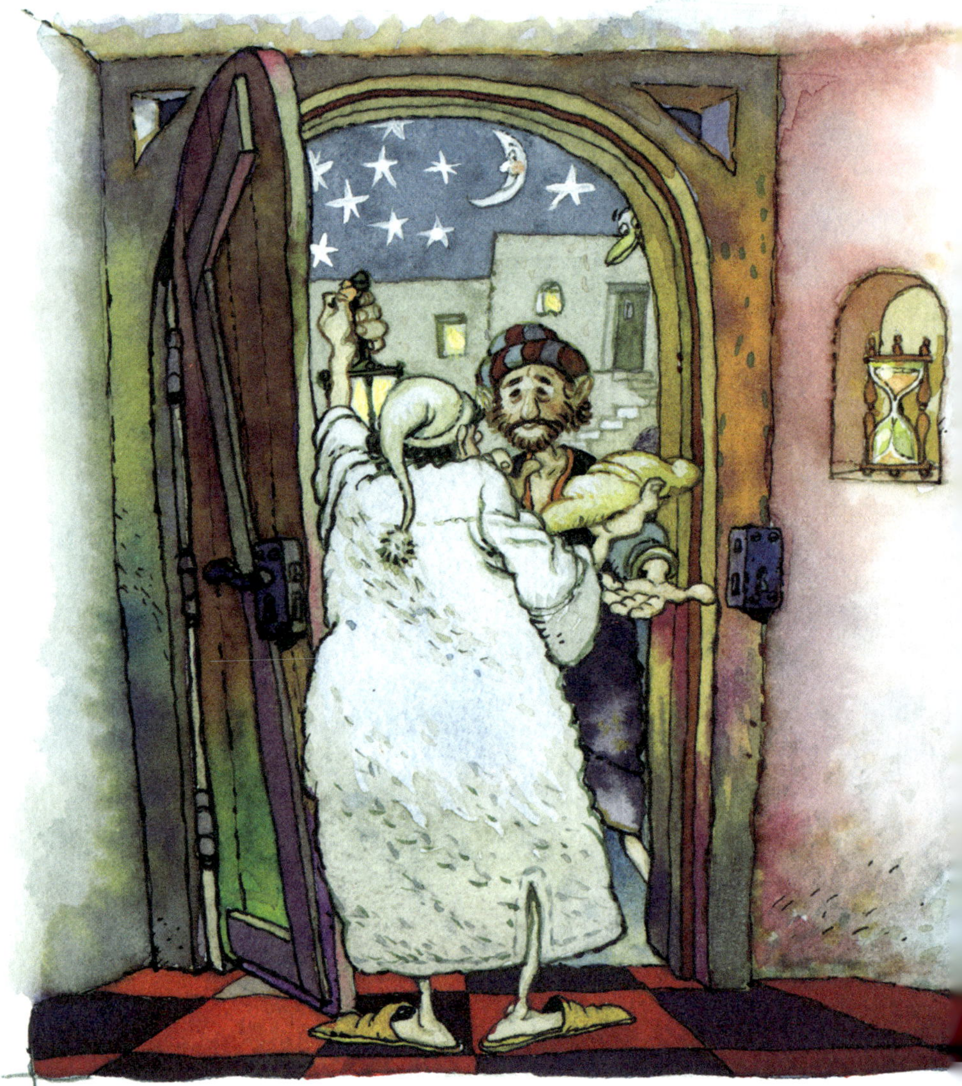

Jesus told another story about a man who kept knocking on his neighbor's door because he needed to borrow some bread for another friend.

What happens when you knock on a door? Try it now. When you pray, it is like knocking on the door to heaven. God always hears your prayers, no matter how softly you whisper them.

Jesus told the story of a young man who wanted more. He wanted more money, more things, more friends, and he wanted to travel more. So he left home. This was a sad day for his father.

What do YOU want more of?

394

Soon the young man ran out of money, so he took a job feeding pigs. But the pigs were getting more food than he was, so he went back home. There his father welcomed him with open arms.

Nothing is more important than the love of God. Can you go hug someone you love?

Children and Jesus

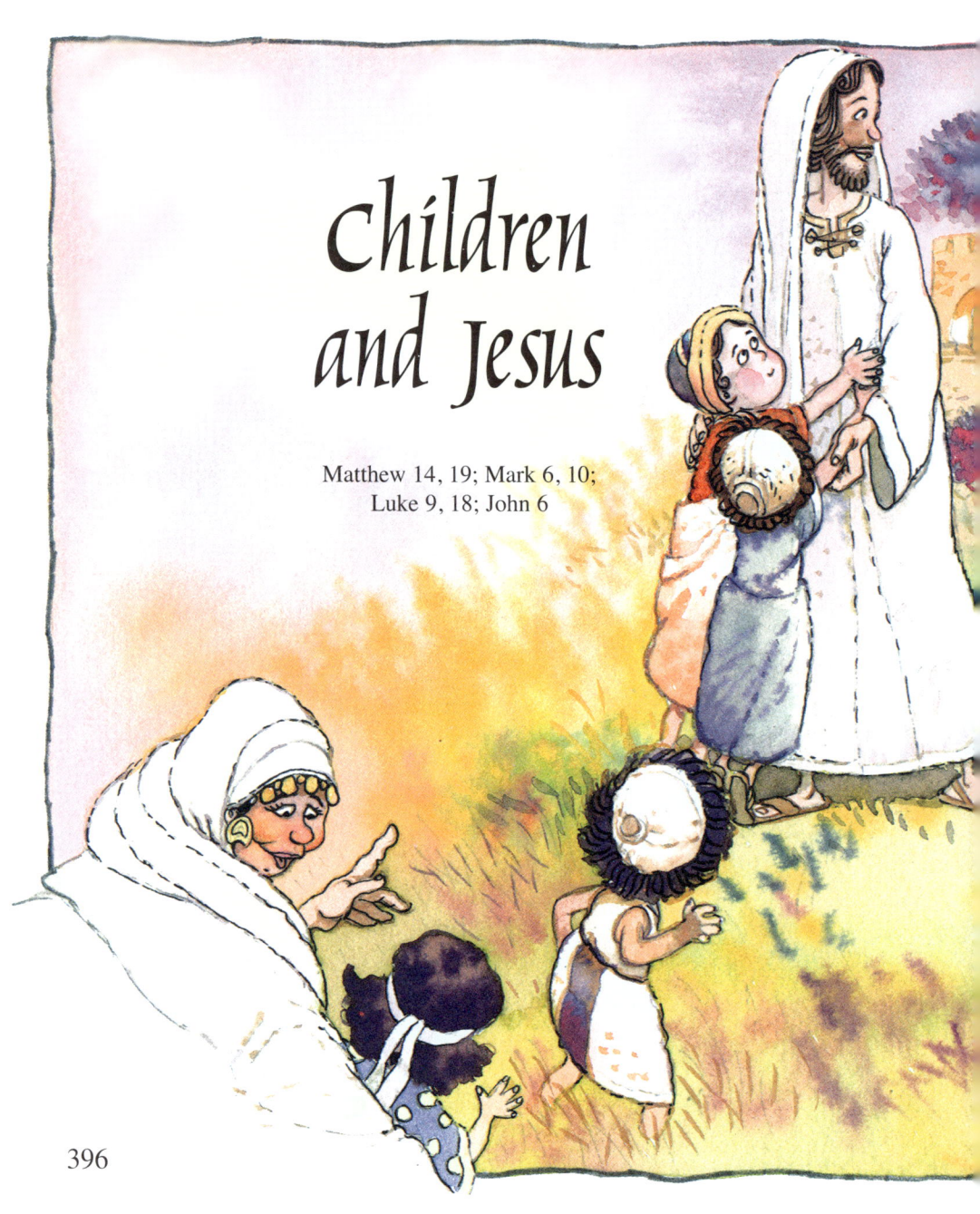

Matthew 14, 19; Mark 6, 10;
Luke 9, 18; John 6

Jesus' friends once told some children, "Go away. Leave Jesus alone!" But Jesus told them, "No! Let the children come to Me."

Jesus liked to teach children of *all* ages. Once, at the end of a long day, Jesus' friends said, "Send everyone home. They're all so hungry." But Jesus said there was more He wanted to teach.

Jesus called, "Who has some food?"
A little boy stepped forward.
"I have some fish and bread, sir.
I will share, but it's not much."

All the people grew still. Jesus looked up. He called out to God and thanked His Father for the food. Then Jesus blessed the bread and broke it into many pieces.

401

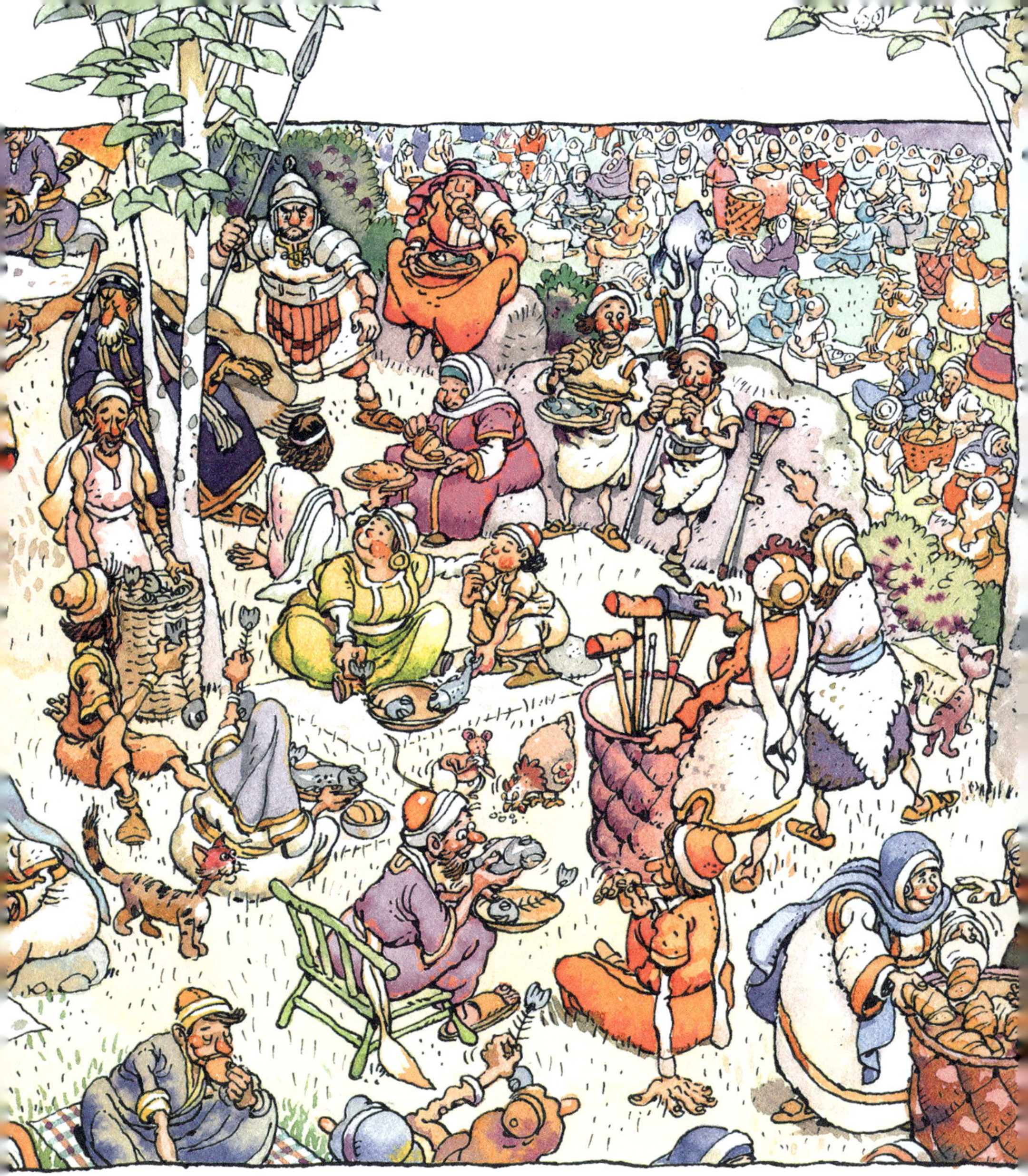

Surprise! There was more bread and more fish, more than enough for everyone! With Jesus' blessing, one little child like you can make a BIG difference.

Jesus in Jerusalem

Matthew 21, 26–27; Mark 11, 14–15;
Luke 19, 22–23; John 12–13, 18

When Jesus entered Jerusalem, the people cheered for Him in a parade. They waved palm branches up and down. Wave your hands. Hooray for Jesus!

The temple leaders did not like Jesus. They paid His disciple Judas thirty pieces of silver to help them trap Jesus.

Why do you think these people didn't like Jesus?

> *At meals we ask God's blessing.
> That means we are thanking God.*

In Jerusalem Jesus thanked God for the bread and wine. He broke the bread into pieces, and passed the bread and wine to His friends.

But Judas led Jesus' enemies right to Jesus. Peter fought back! He cut off the ear of a guard. Jesus teaches us to love our enemies. He picked up the ear and made it better.

Jesus taught that we should not hurt people—even when we are angry.

Peter was scared after the guards took Jesus away. They asked him, "You know Jesus, don't you?" But he said, "No!" three times! After the third time, he heard the rooster crow. Then Peter remembered . . . Jesus had told him, "You will deny me three times before the rooster crows." Peter was very sad.

What did the rooster sound like?

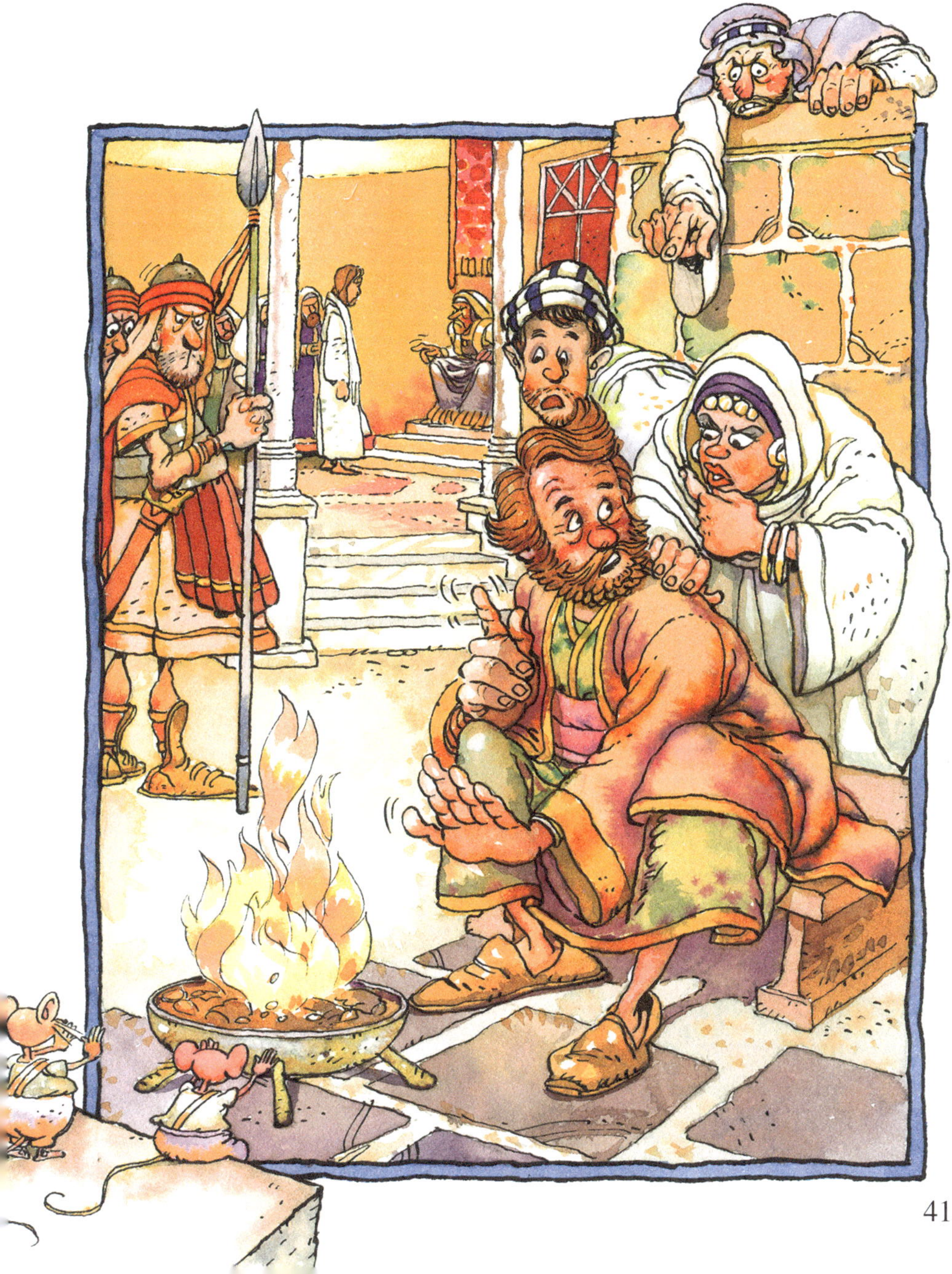

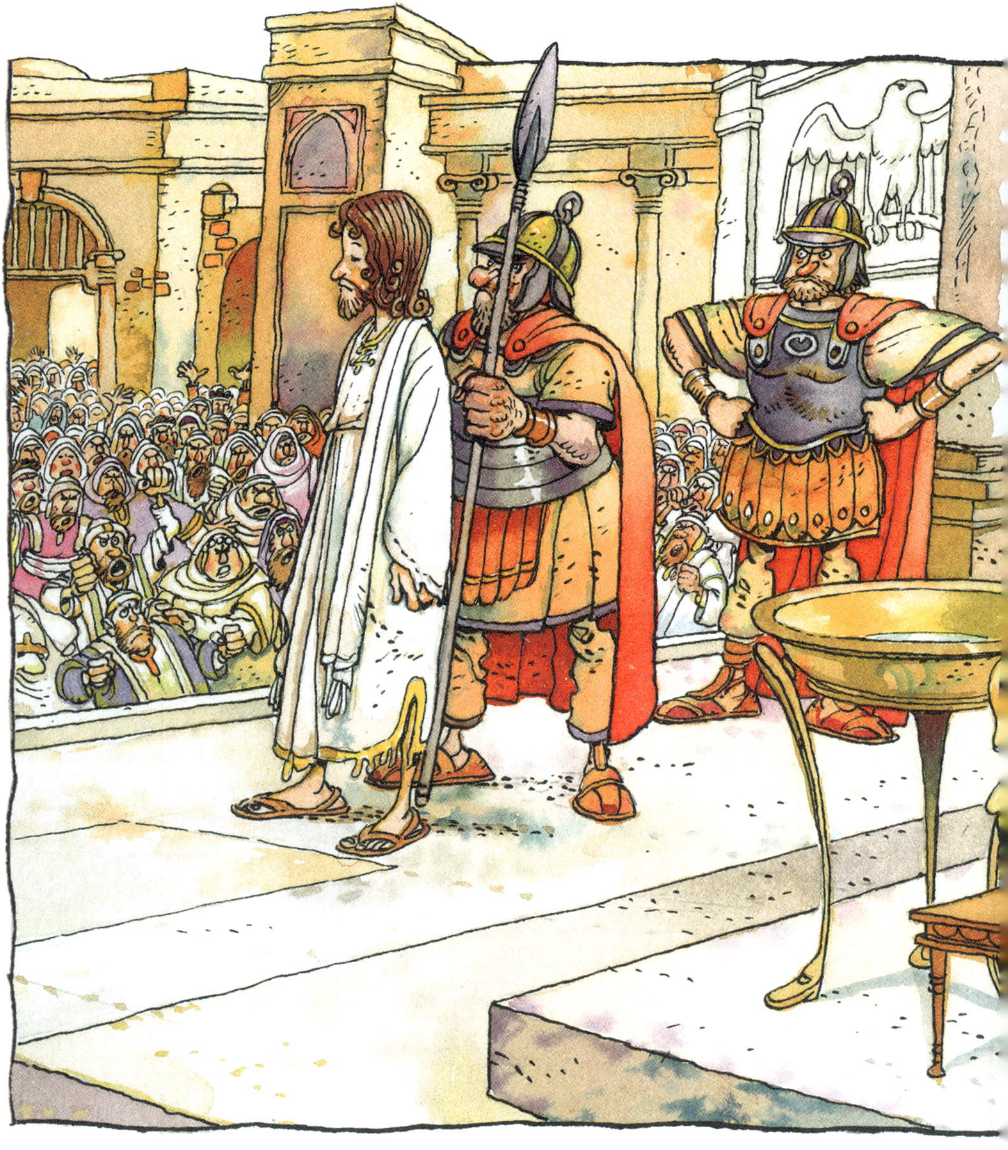

Jesus' enemies brought Him before a judge. "Kill Him on the cross!" they screamed. What terrible words Jesus' enemies said! Did Jesus do anything wrong? Did He get angry at His enemies? No!

The First Easter

Matthew 27–28; Mark 15–16; Luke 23–24; John 14, 19–21; Acts 1

417

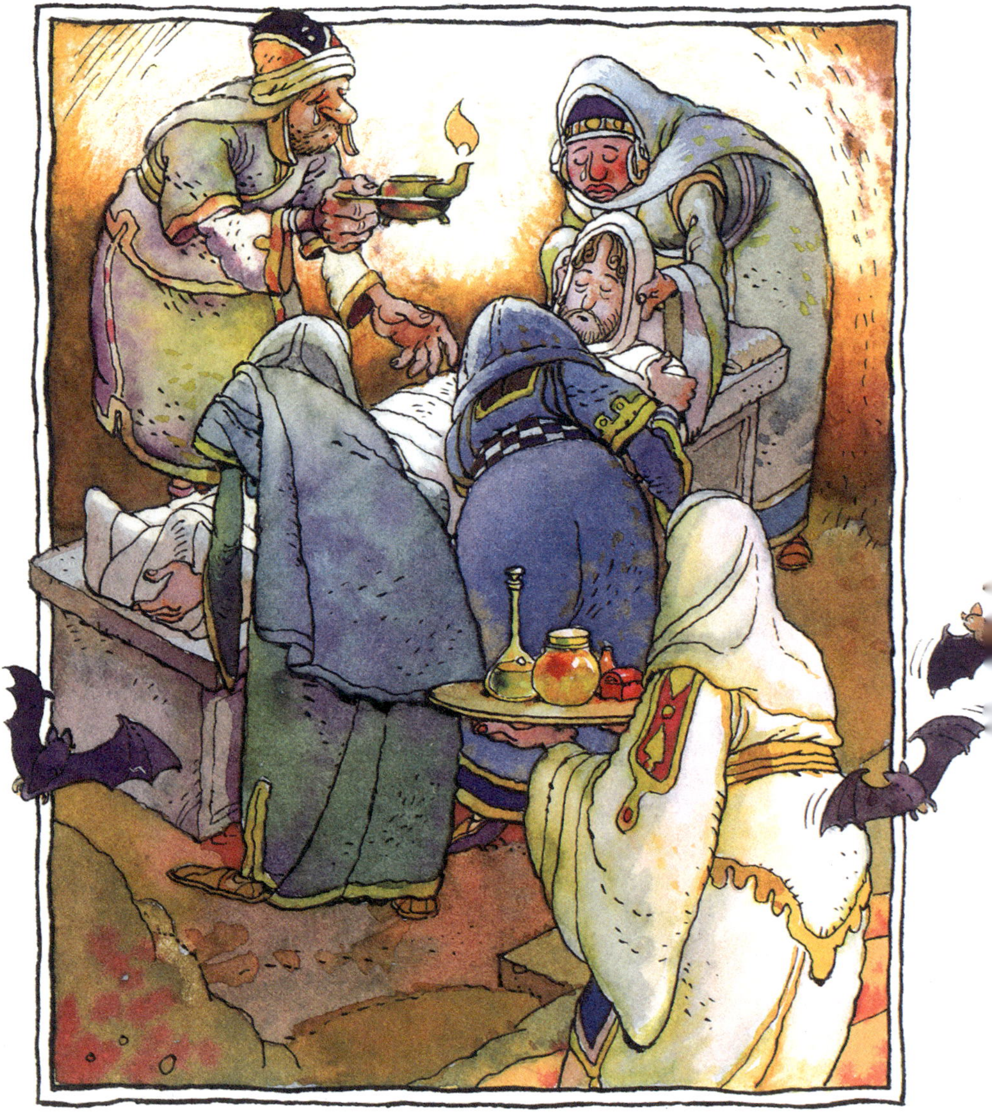

Jesus' enemies nailed Him to a cross, where He died. His friends and family were crying and very sad. They took Him down off the cross, and placed Him gently in a special cave, with guards outside.

This story is about new life through Jesus. When Jesus died, everything seemed very dark—just like it will be inside my cocoon.

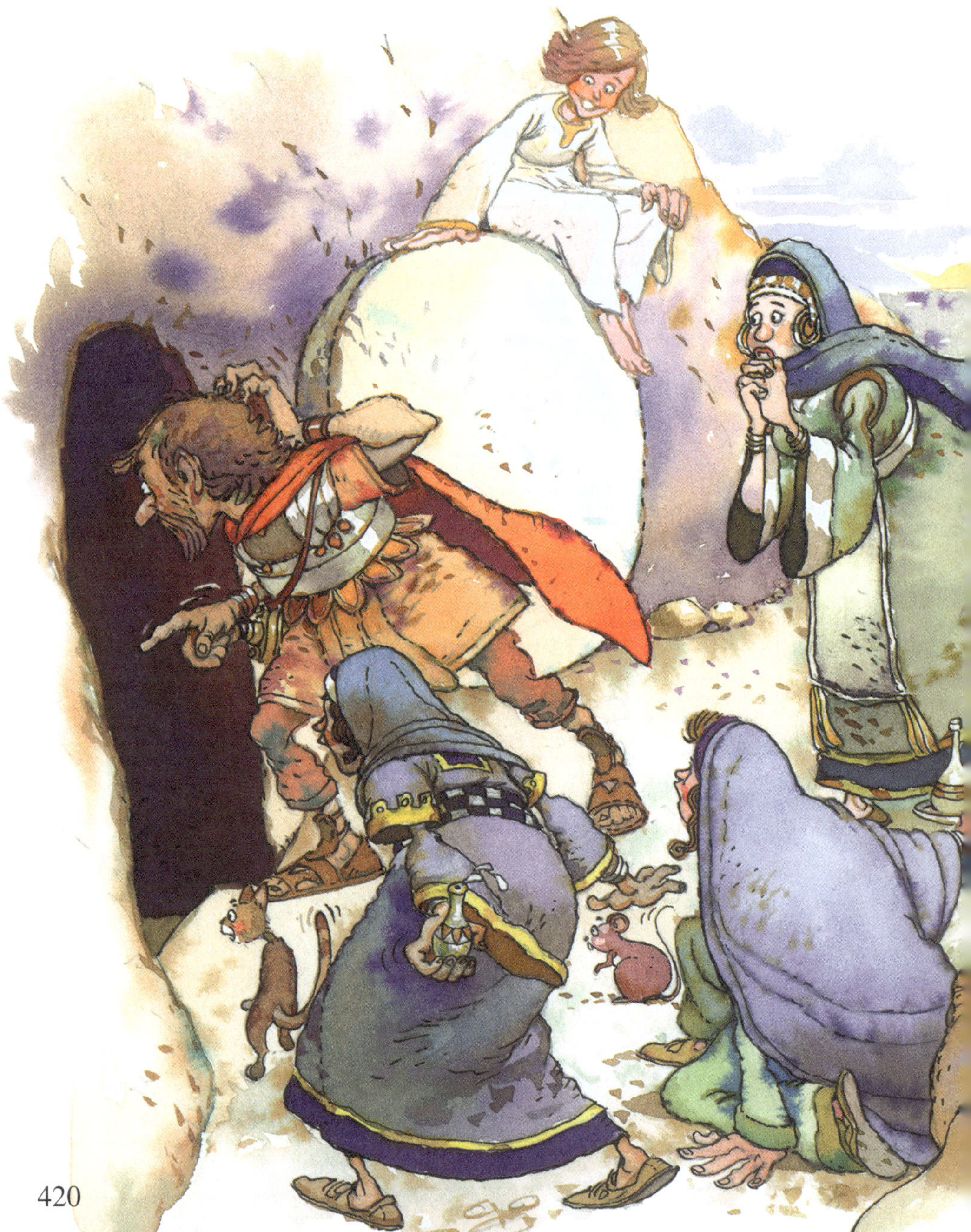

A few days later, Jesus' friends came back to the cave. It was empty! "Where is Jesus?" they cried. The guards didn't know anything.

See if you can find signs of the miracle of new life outside: a tiny tree, a flower, the morning sun.

An angel said, "Fear not. Are you looking for Jesus? Jesus is alive again! He's not dead! Be happy! Go in and look where He used to lie. Now, go tell everyone that He's alive." The women ran off, hardly believing their eyes and ears.

Look at what happened to me! Do you think it was a miracle? On which holiday do we remember this story?

423

After Jesus rose from the dead, He visited His friends who were fishing and said, "Throw your net out again!" Then they caught so many fish, the net almost burst!

Which season is Easter in? Not winter, autumn, or summer! SPRING! Spring is the time for baby lambs and butterflies. It is a time for new life. We have new life when we believe in Jesus and follow Him.

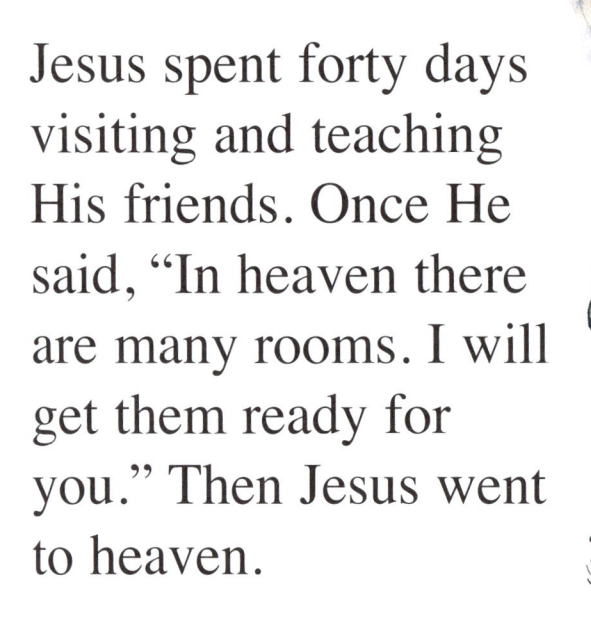

Jesus spent forty days visiting and teaching His friends. Once He said, "In heaven there are many rooms. I will get them ready for you." Then Jesus went to heaven.

How many rooms does your home have? How many signs of new life can you think of? Now thank God for each one of them.

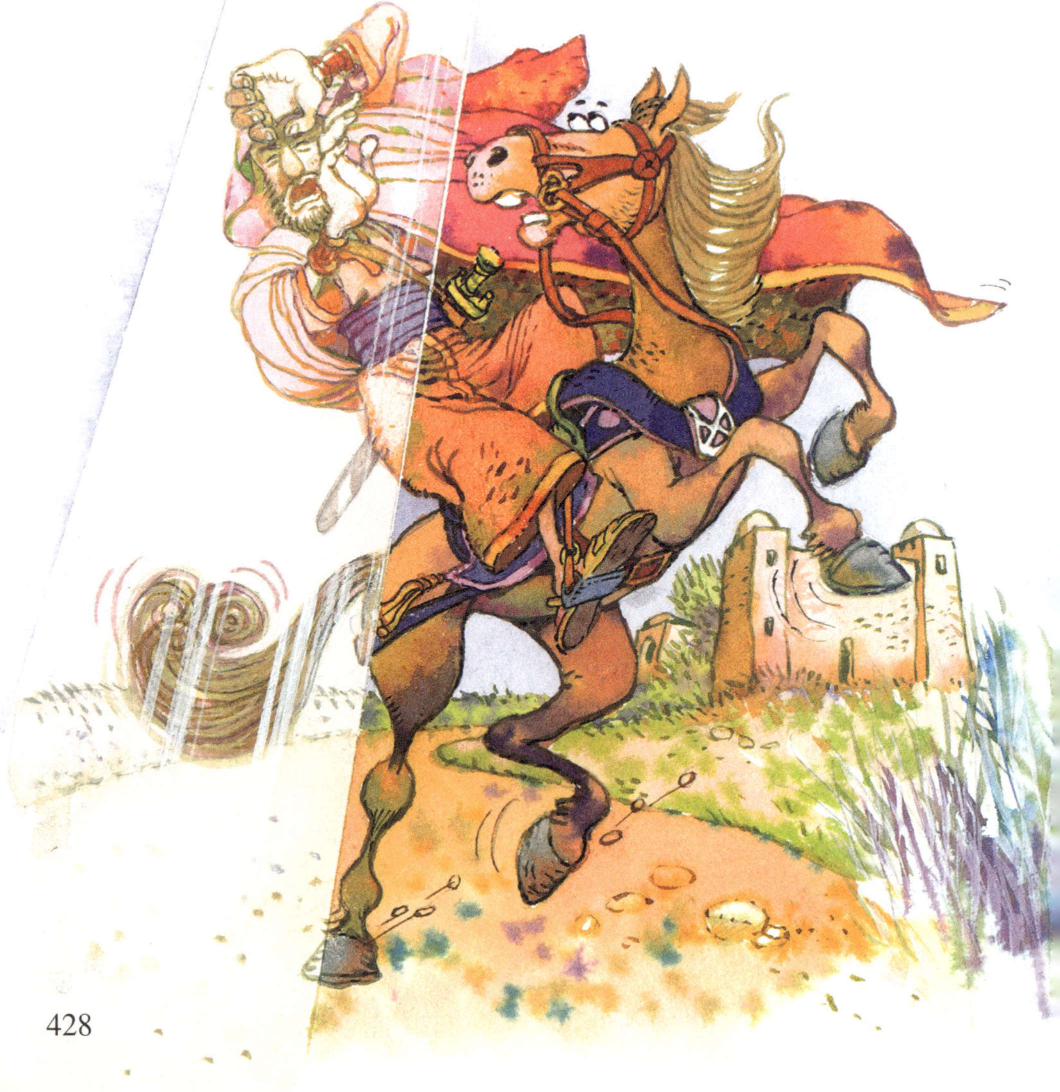

Paul's Change of Heart

Acts 7–9, 11, 13–28; Epistles of Paul

Don't look now, but this is Saul.

Saul used to hurt Jesus' friends until a bright light blinded him.

Saul heard Jesus' voice say, "When you hurt My followers, you hurt Me." Then God helped Saul see that Jesus is the Son of God.

431

When Jesus helped Saul to see again, He gave Saul a new name. From then on he was called Paul. After his change of heart, Paul traveled far and wide, telling everyone he met about Jesus' love.

Greece and Turkey are two of the countries Paul visited. Can you find them on a map?

The more Paul talked to people about Jesus, the more often Jesus' enemies arrested and hurt Paul.

During his many years in jail, Paul wrote several letters to his friends. He taught of Jesus and God's love.

Does your family write letters?

God Promises a New World

Matthew 4, 10; Mark 1, 3; Luke 5–6; John 1;
Revelation 1, 3, 17–22

John was a follower of Jesus.

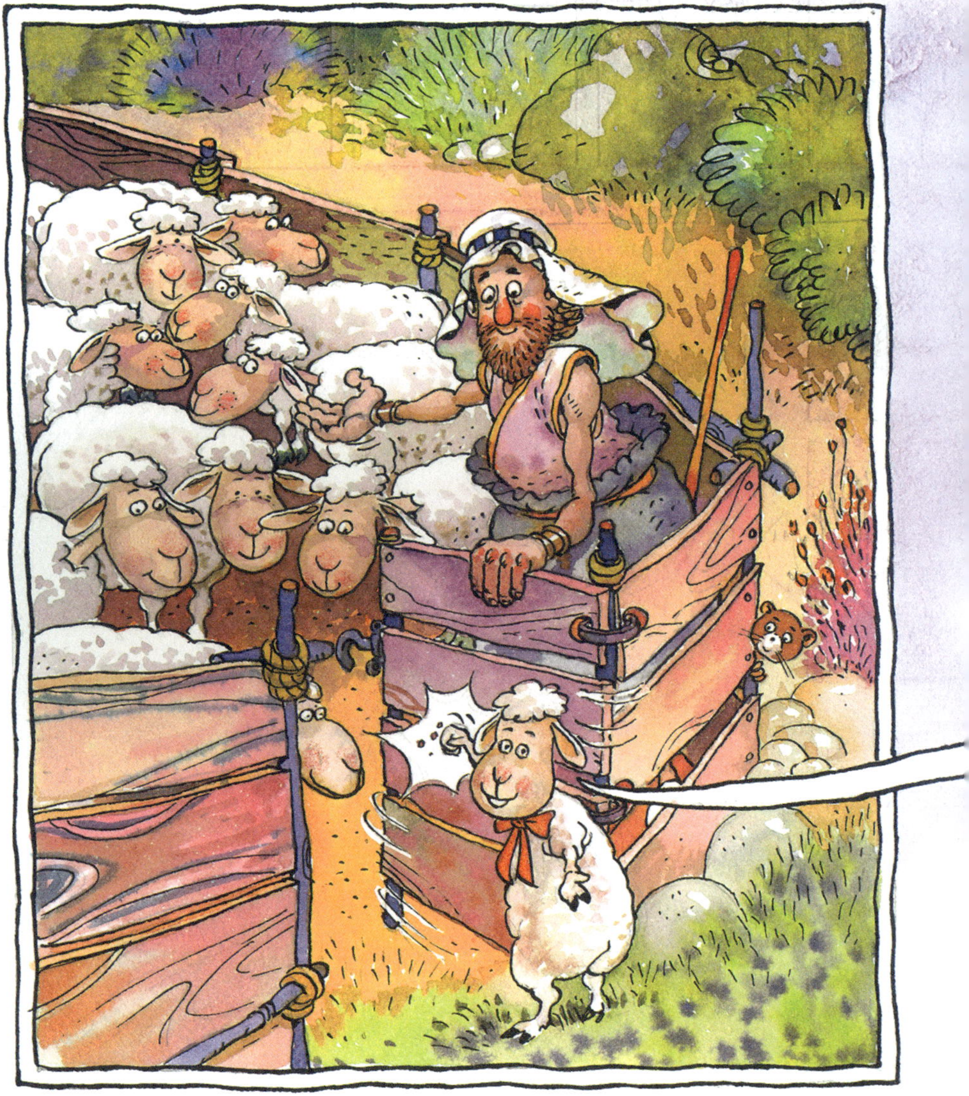

When John was an old man, he had a vision, which was a special message from God. He wrote down Jesus' words, "I'm here for anyone who asks Me into their lives. I'm standing at the door, knocking, waiting for them to hear My voice and open the door."

Go to the door, close it, then have the person reading to you knock on it. Opening the door and letting them in is like asking Jesus into your own heart.

In John's vision, he heard music and saw a huge crowd, the followers of Jesus from all time and all countries. No one could count all the people!

Try counting all the people in this picture. Can you find me, the little lamb?

441

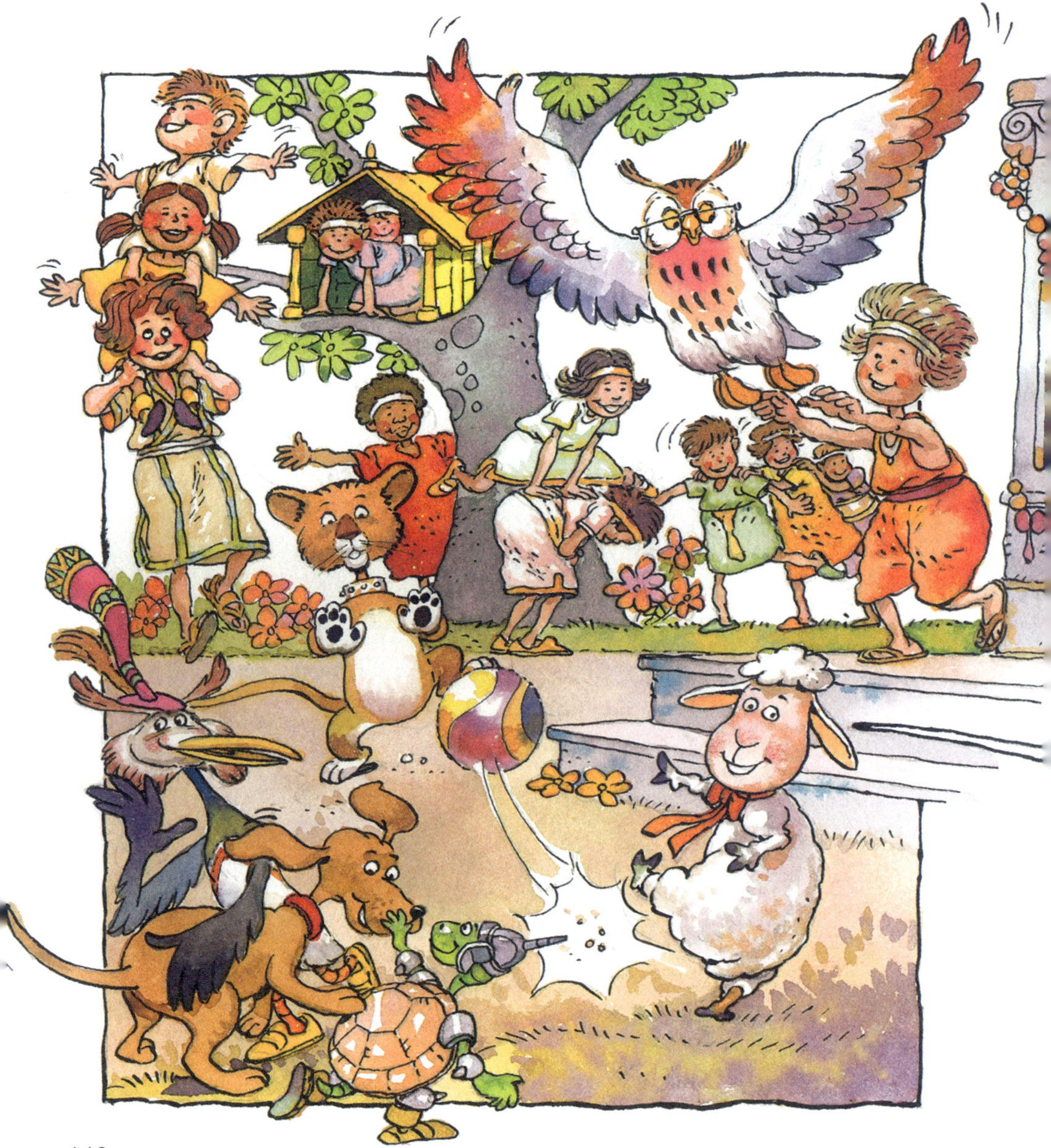

John's vision of heaven shows us what God's kingdom will be like. There will be no more bad people, and no more sadness.

Name three things you think heaven will be like.

In John's vision he saw that those who had chosen to follow Jesus were there with God. He said heaven was a place of light and happiness.

John wrote often about light, living in the light, and God's kingdom as a place of light. Turn the light on and off now. Who is the Light of the world?

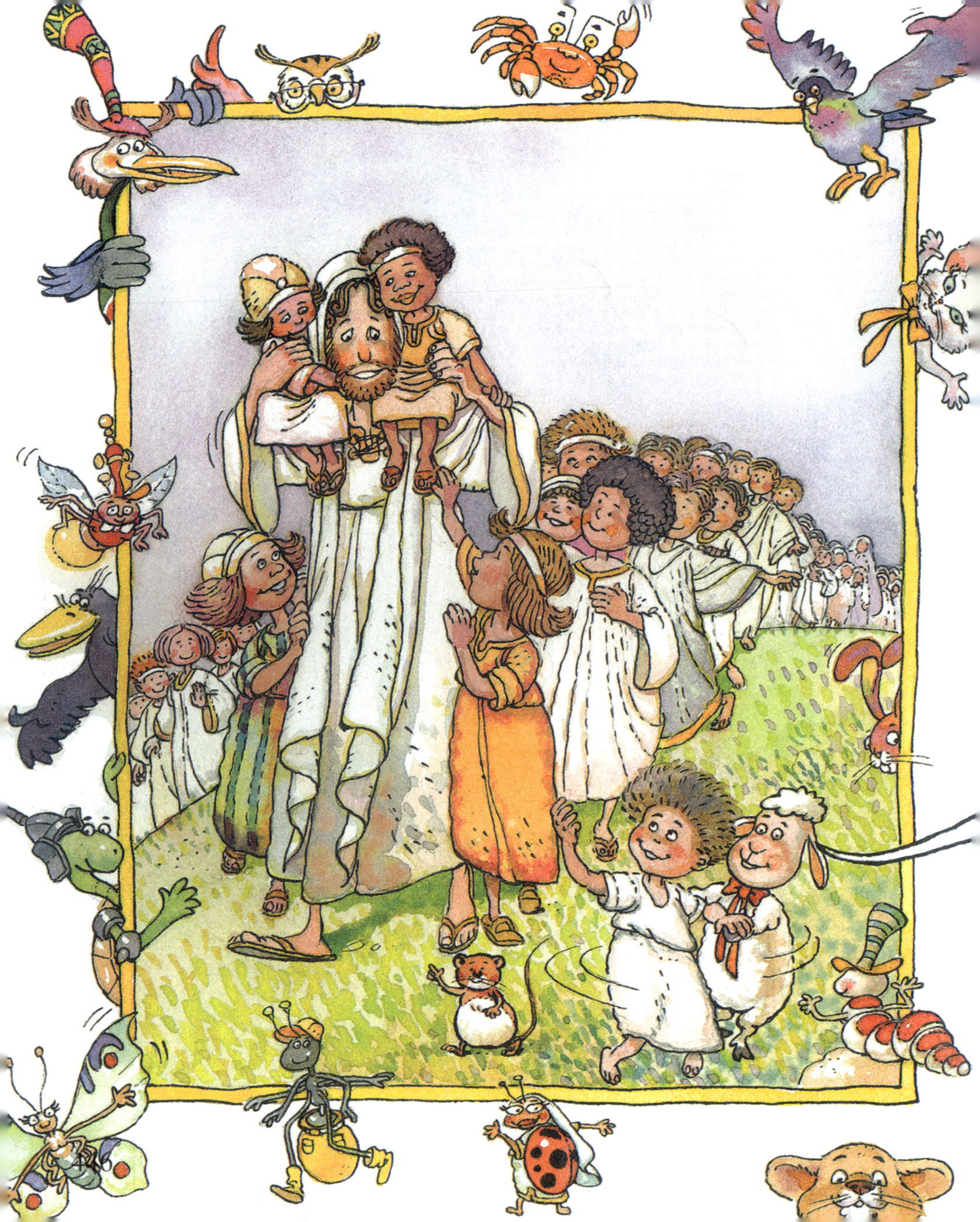

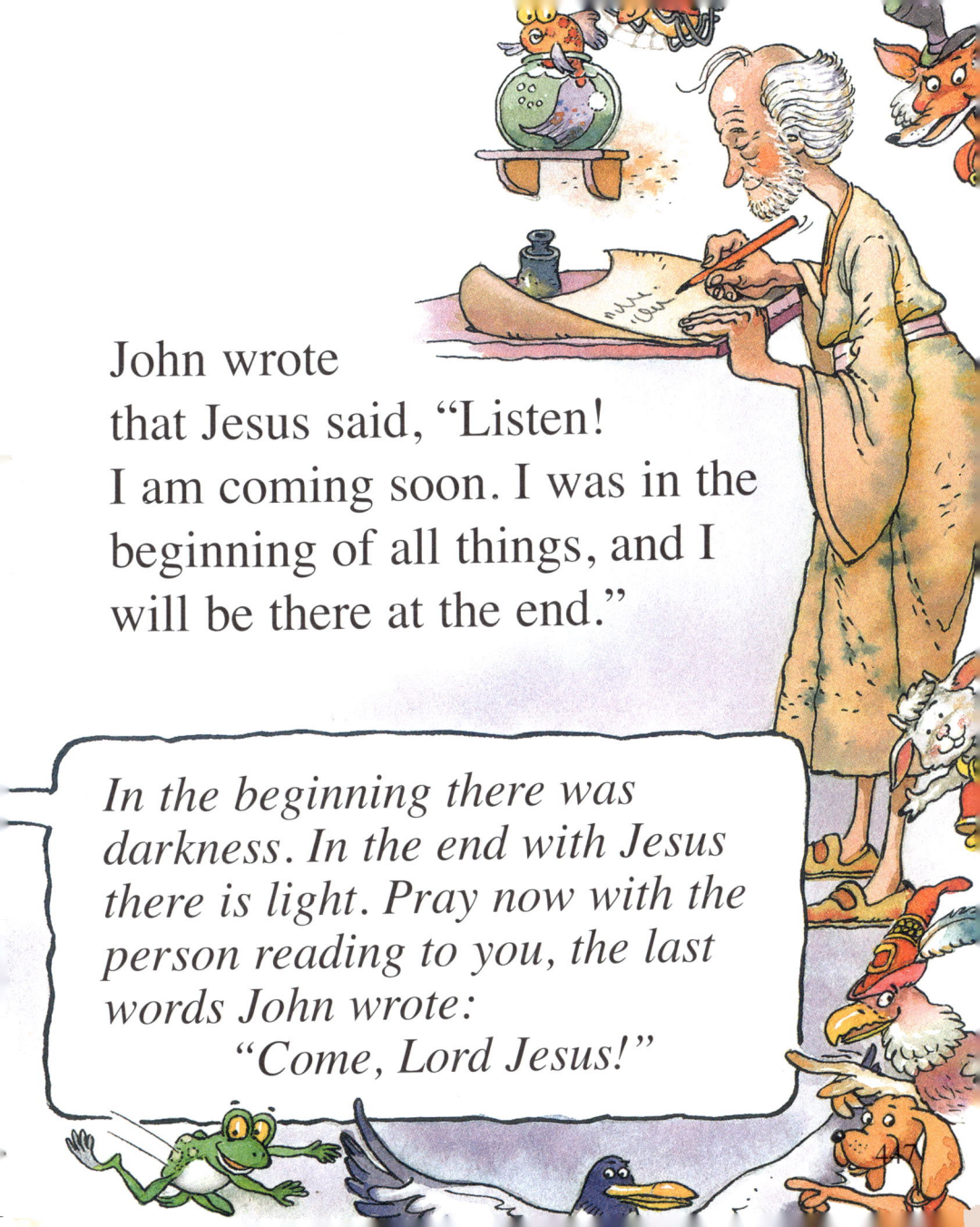

John wrote that Jesus said, "Listen! I am coming soon. I was in the beginning of all things, and I will be there at the end."

In the beginning there was darkness. In the end with Jesus there is light. Pray now with the person reading to you, the last words John wrote:
  "Come, Lord Jesus!"

About the Illustrator:
José Pérez Montero is an award-winning illustrator and painter who has illustrated more than seventy children's books. He started selling his paintings at the age of thirteen, and has studied at the San Fernando and Circulo Schools of Fine Arts in Madrid. His landscape and portrait paintings have hung in numerous exhibitions throughout Spain. During the last thirty years he has drawn illustrations for comics, advertising, and textbooks, but he is best known for his illustrations of children's books, which have been published in over forty countries. His work was selected for exhibition at the Society of Illustrators' "Illustrator 38" exhibition 1993–1998. He lives in Spain with his wife, two sons, and grandchildren.

About the Author:
Since 1987, Anne de Graaf has traveled extensively in eastern Europe and sub-Saharan Africa, including Mozambique, Namibia, Zimbabwe, Botswana, and Tanzania. She has written more than eighty books, which have sold more than five million copies worldwide and been translated into more than fifty languages. Her Hidden Harvest series has sold in seven countries. The final book of the series, *Out of the Red Shadow*, won the Christy Award 2000 for International Historical Fiction. Anne de Graaf has also worked as a journalist for the Dutch National Press Agency, and as an economics translator for the Dutch government. Born in San Francisco and a graduate of Stanford University, she has lived for the past twenty years in Ireland and the Netherlands with her husband and their two children.

During the 1999 Frankfurt World Book Fair, both José Pérez Montero and Anne de Graaf were awarded the East European Christian Literature Award.